...and now you want me to do what?..

The lost poems, art, and photos of Julie Cason

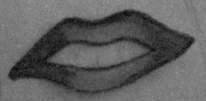

CORY CASON

Take some time to wonder why
The time has seemed to
Fly right by
All days and nights
Into one
And the work is never
Done
Be it mundane
Or sometimes a nice
Surprise in their eyes
No time to waste behind
My eyes
To discover
Take some time to wonder why
The time has seemed to
Fly right by
All days and nights
Into one
And the work is never
Done
Be it mundane
Or sometimes a nice
Surprise in their eyes
No time to waste behind
My eyes
To discover

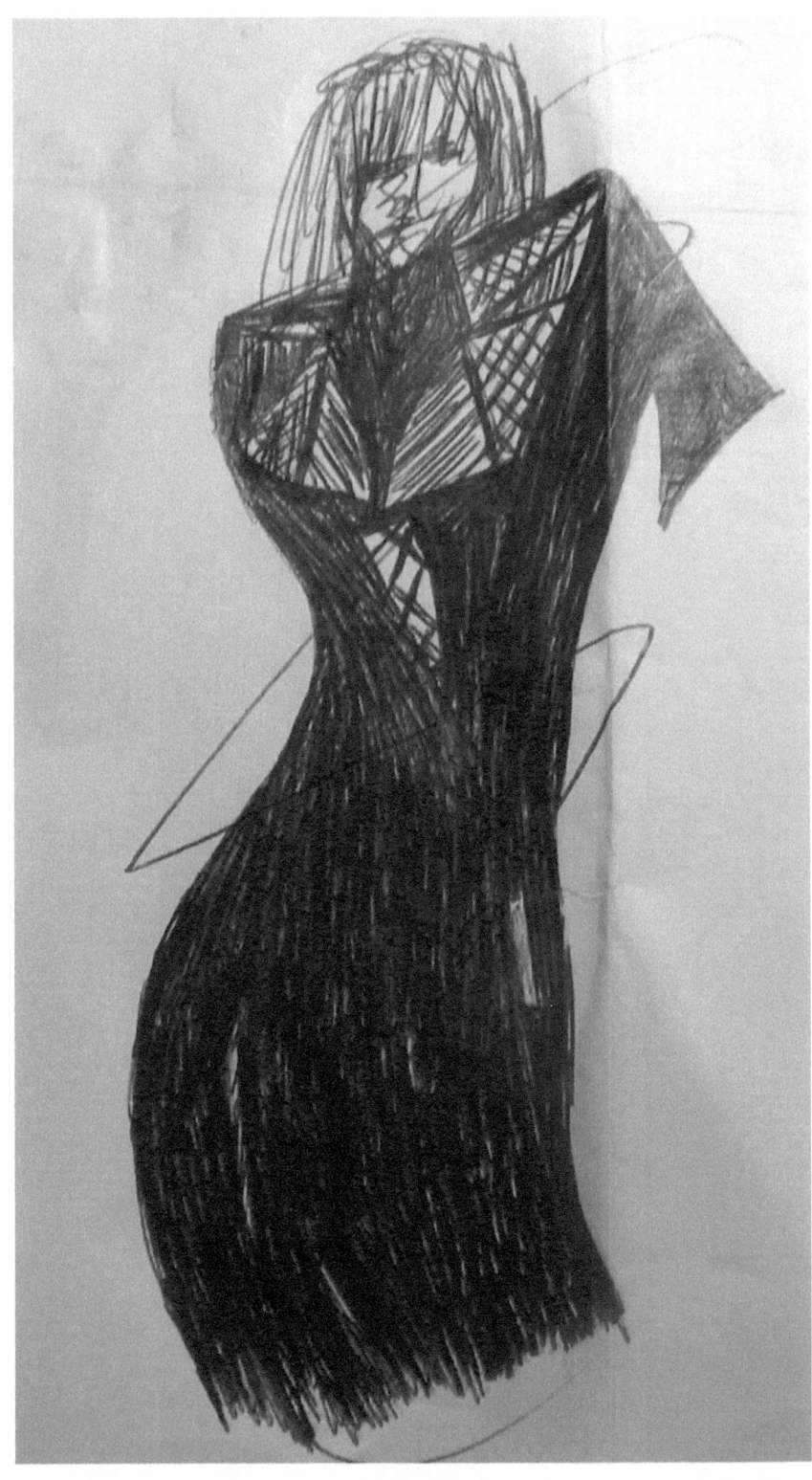

Change the
        Name and change
            The face even change
                The time and place
                    Do what you will but
                        It will still be the same
                            Because you can't
                    change
                                The mind in
                    either
                                    Shape or
                        space

Take a look
At the movie playing
Behind your eyes
When they're closed
And you can't see

Nothing is easy
And nothing is free
And I'm trying to live
This life
With just me
No guidance
No knowledge
No time
And I'm afraid all
The answers
Aren't easy to find
But I'm still gonna keep
On taking my time
And let everything
Go here and go there
Til you don't have a line
To pay for anything for you
To pay me
And then maybe I'll
Tell you what I
Wanna be
In this life

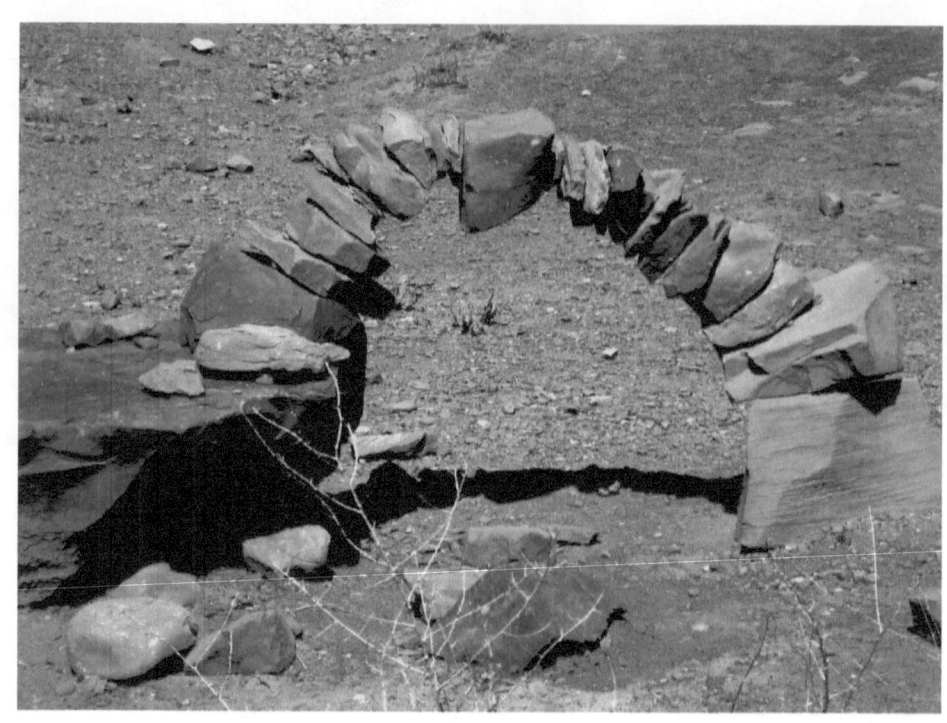

Under a blanket
Of Sky
Of blue and
Red
Changing
The times of day

Take away the whispers
And the cold dark nights
Smother out the shadows
Touch my soul with light
Take away the whispers
And the cold dark nights
Smother out the shadows
Touch my soul with light

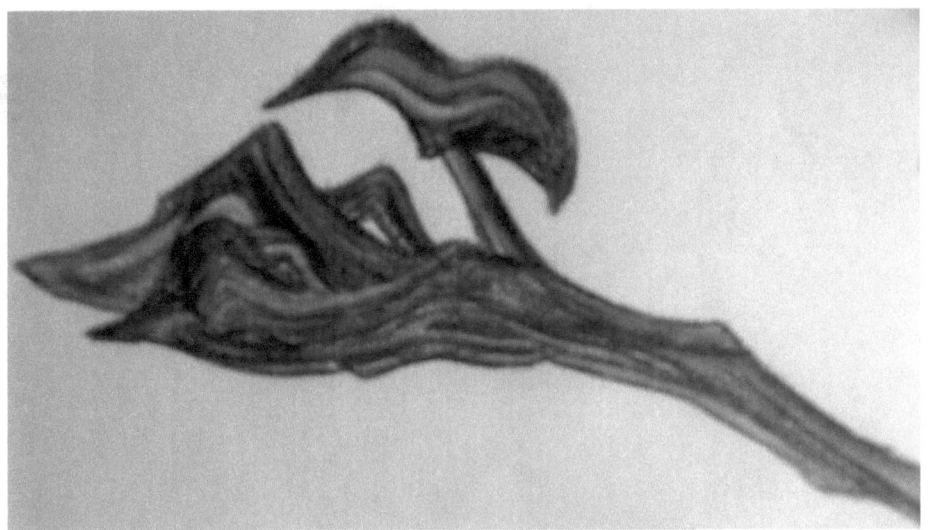

Follow the line
Down one more time
To the place where
The pastures are
Ablaze with fire

So many tales
Still left to tell
Somewhere along the way
To many ears to

Misconstrue every word
Let the confusion among
The little people
Overflow and take
Away from the truth
In the telling
Someday I won't have
To tell them alone
Because the will
Be part of the past
The characters
Long to
Remember
And not
Forget

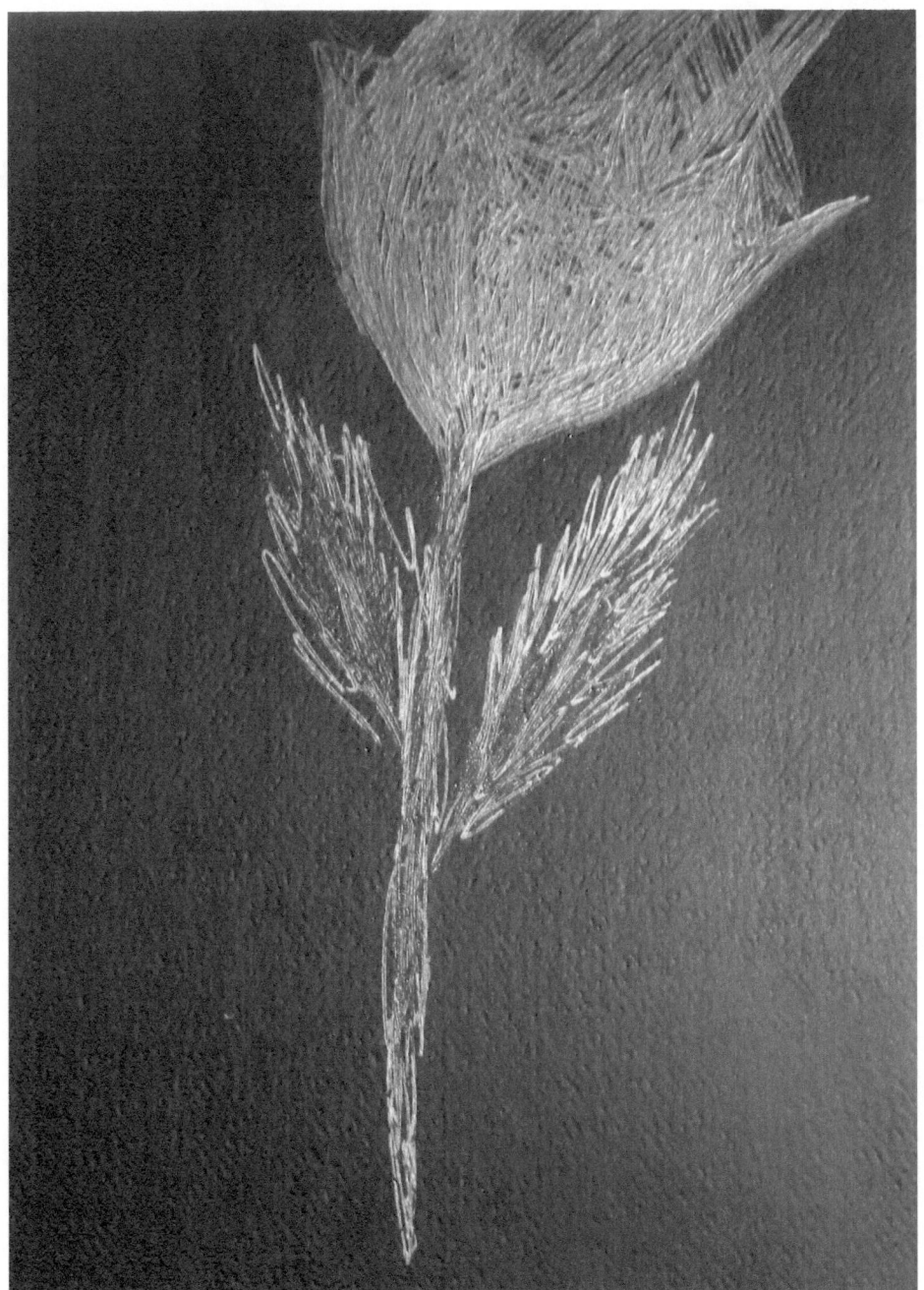

A newborn
Hope
Unjaded
By years
A newborn
Hope
Unjaded
By years

Take a long
Ride home after
The race is no longer
A sport and the
Circus is no more
Wander the boardwalk
Take the Ferris wheel til it stops
Way up high make no more
Memories to take a moment
Away from this
So the vision to
Reach your child's eyes
Will be your vision
On the sky

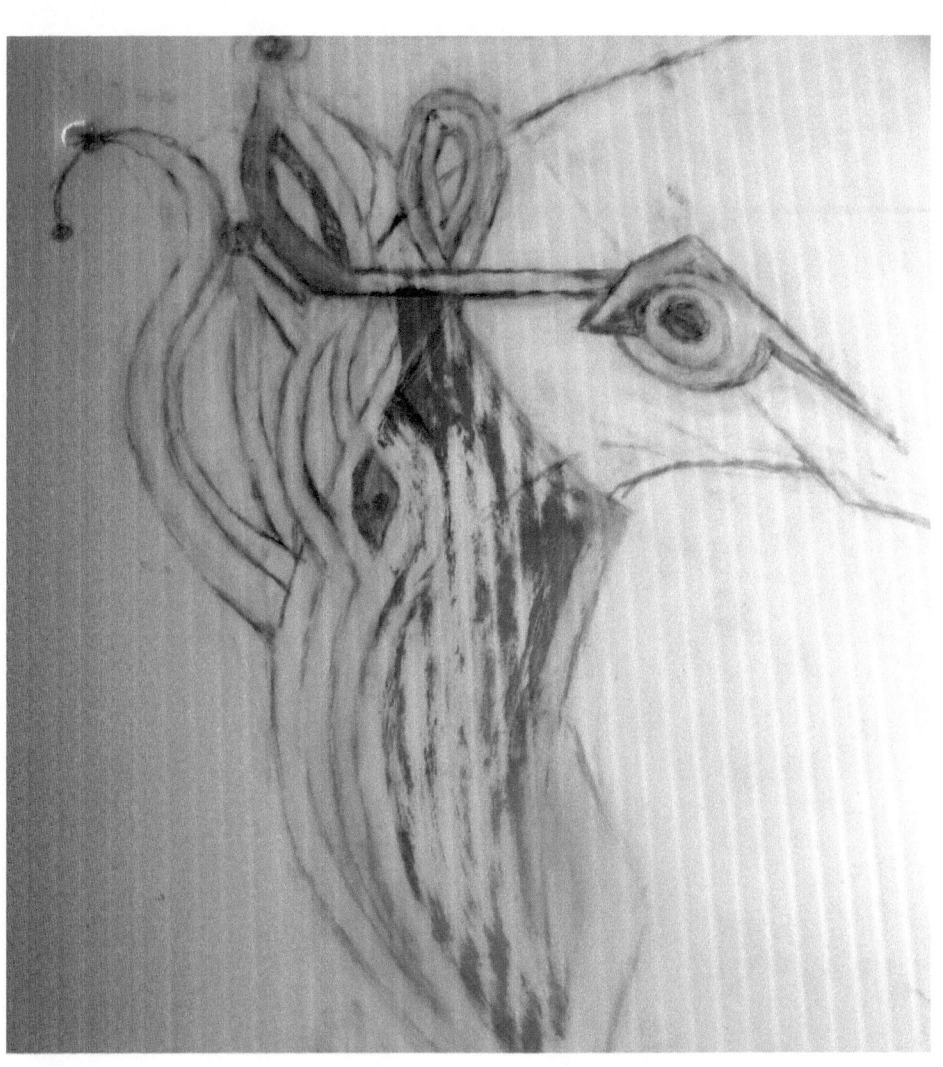

Making shadows
In the flame
Rise figurines
Playful
Terrible things
Each bears a fuel all its own
And all of them
Crave to roam
Among the peoples
Who have brought
Them to life
Knowing that it will last
Just one night
Their little tirade
And mischief in sight

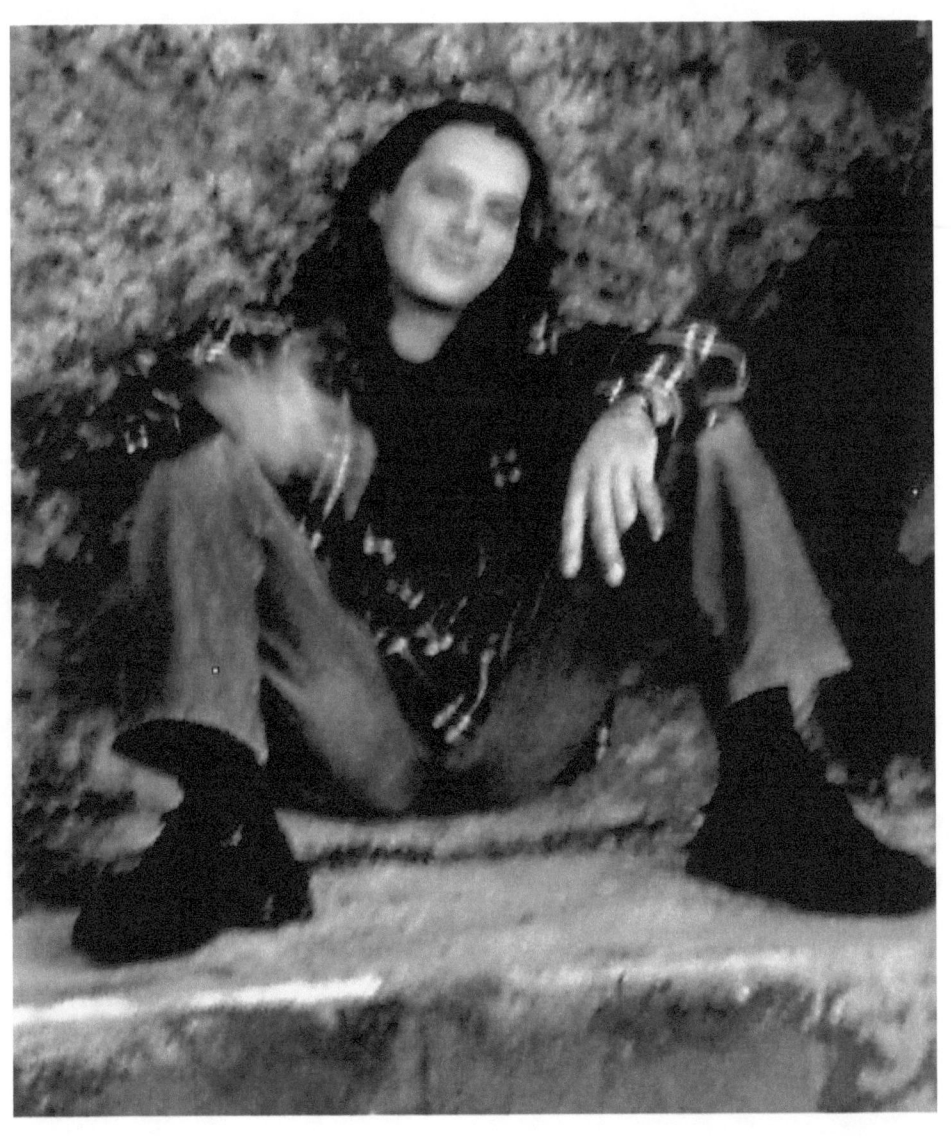

Well if the
Neighborhood let you in
I might decide to stay
I want to watch you dream
So I can hear you scream
My name inside your head

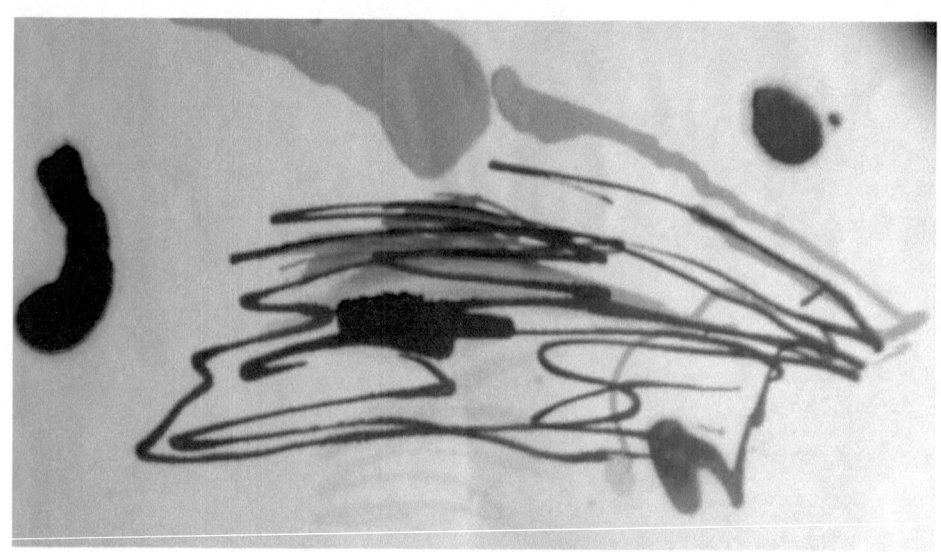

Only a night ago
Quietly surviving
Only a night ago
Dreaming
Only a dream ago
Shining star
Only a dream ago
Hope

Never again will I go from one bar to another
Until the invading monster disintegrate me
This is far more beautiful
Here you disintegrate thoughts
The words are like a galaxy
Of thousands and thousands
Of stars all in a row
And you created them all
Yourself they emerge from
Nothingness and obediently
Return to the nothingness
As soon as new words replace them
It is the dance itself
Devouring moons
Swallowing themselves
Whole fattening on it's
Own absence like a cheesier cat black hole
Beliefs come about
And if two things don't fit
But you believe both of them
Thinking that somewhere hidden
There must be a
Third thing that ties them together
That's not cruelly killing curiosity
Not killing it

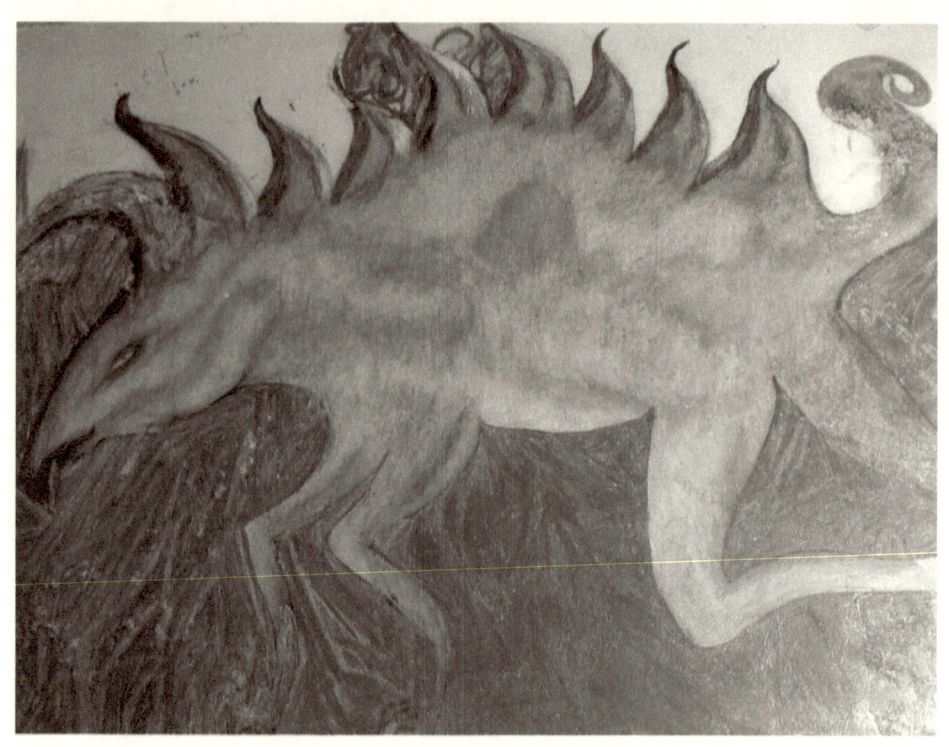

Keeper of the veil
How do you pretend
If you can't see the
Fear you guard

Take away all the
Ugly shapes
In my way
Make them go away
Make them go away
Take away all the
Ugly shapes
In my way
Make them go away
Make them go away

Will you
Say a prayer
For me
Or will you hide inside
Your safe, guarded life
No matter what you do
I still
Will do as I please
And hope to catch you
As you pass
Me through the daily grind
And say just once to you
I'm waiting
For you to do what's right

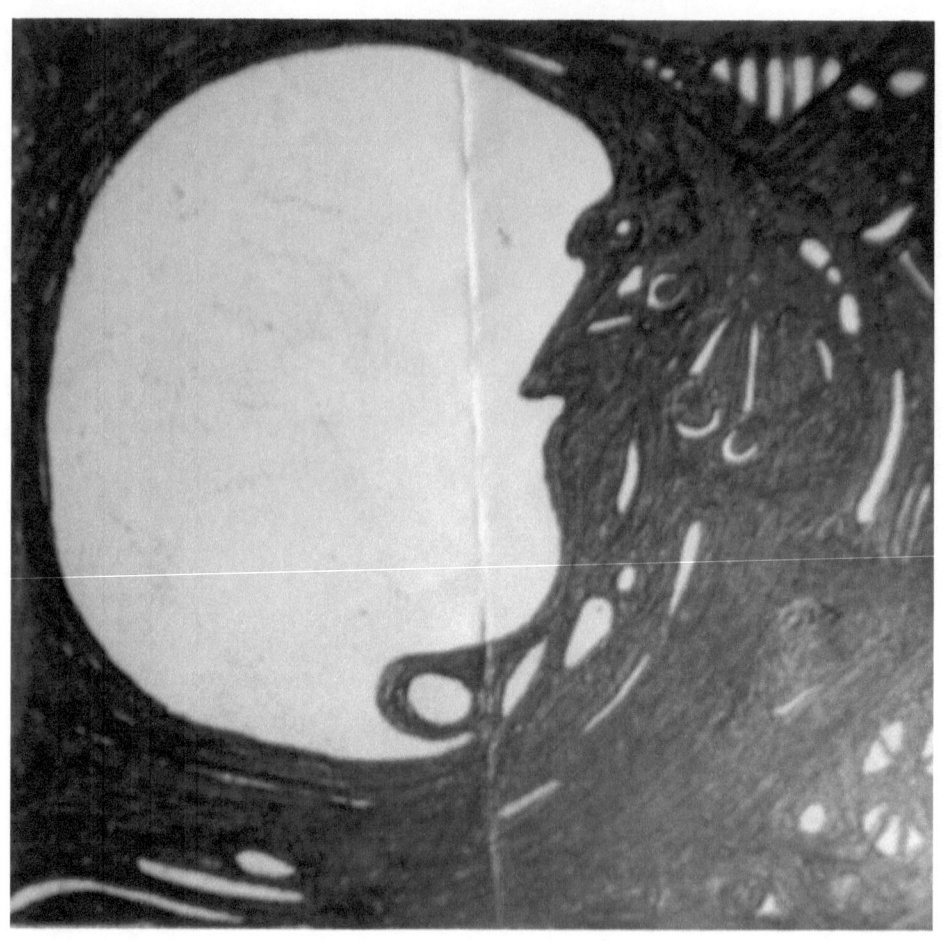

Oh my, oh my
Take a star from the sky
Make it shine all day
And all night
But keep it out of sight
When the moon is full

Waiting the surf
Subsides
To make an effort
In healing

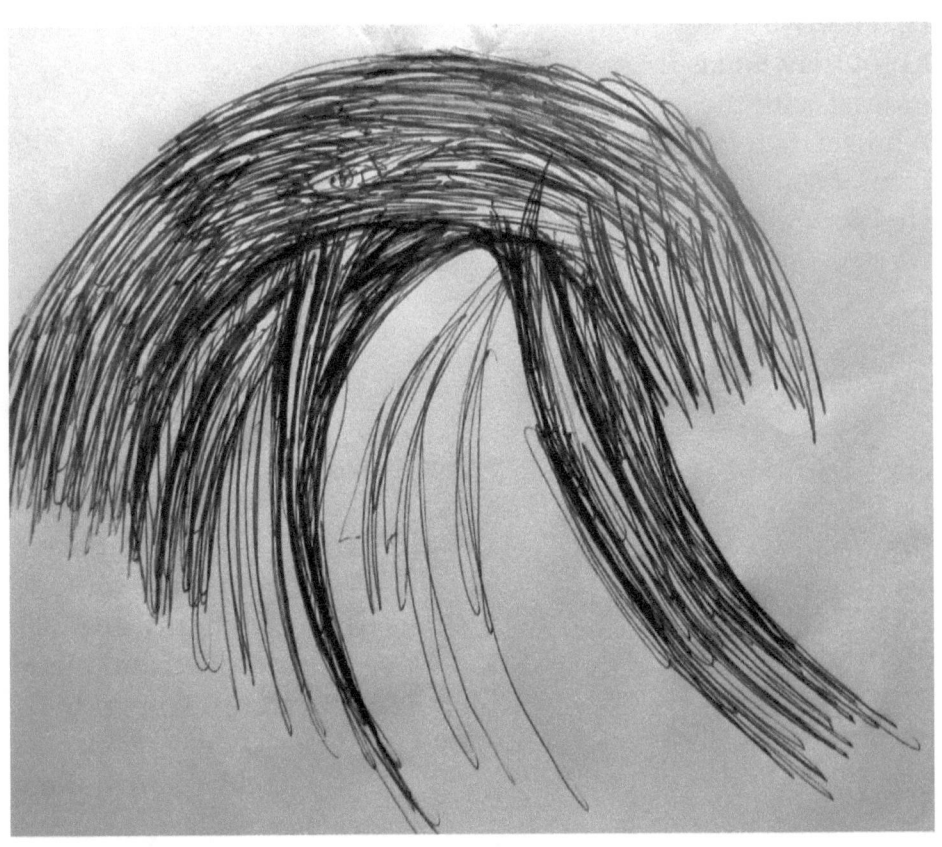

Oh no home to go to
He thinks he's going to be
In a show
Of non-affection more
Mental abjection
Until I finally adhere
To be loose of this affectionate
Slap in the face
That is always done with
Absolutely no taste
At least with the one
Who wears this face
Cannot stand it when he plays
This person

I will not give in
I will not lose sight
I will not make everything
For you alright
I will never leave
I will never fade
Until my goal has
Been fulfilled and made
Exactly as I want it to be
I am you
And you are not me

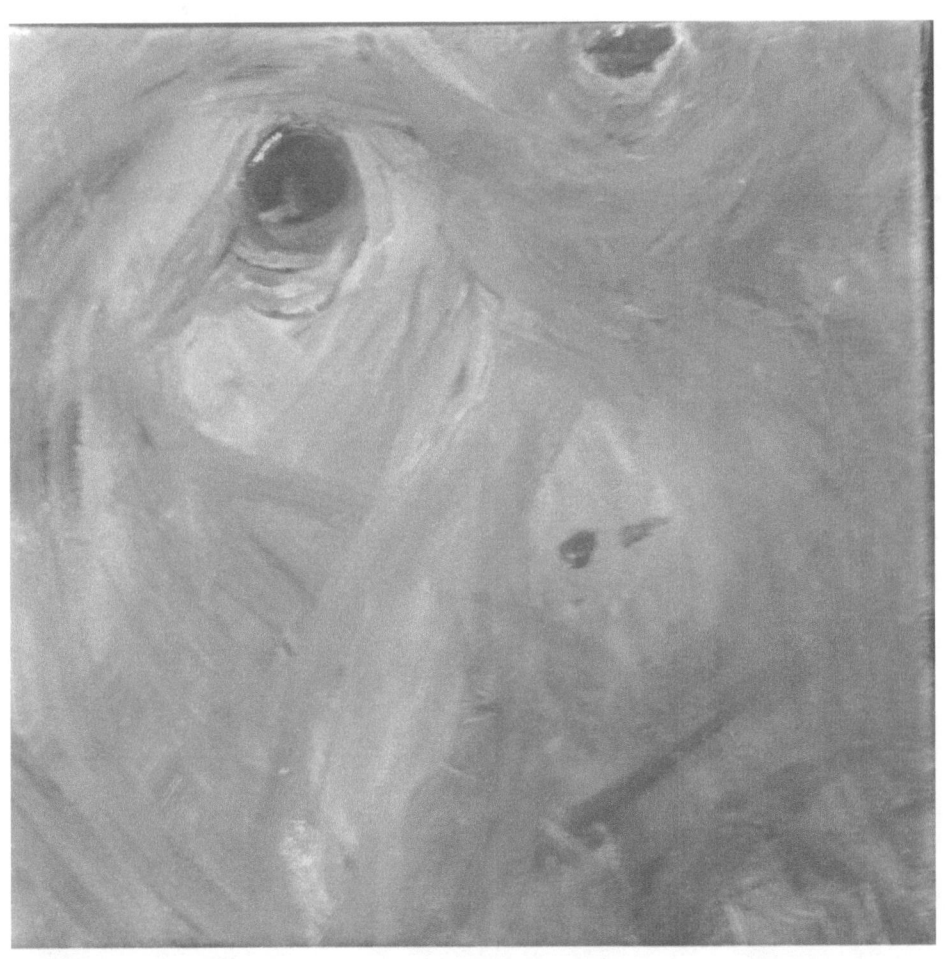

Watchful
Deciding
Exactly what
To share
With you

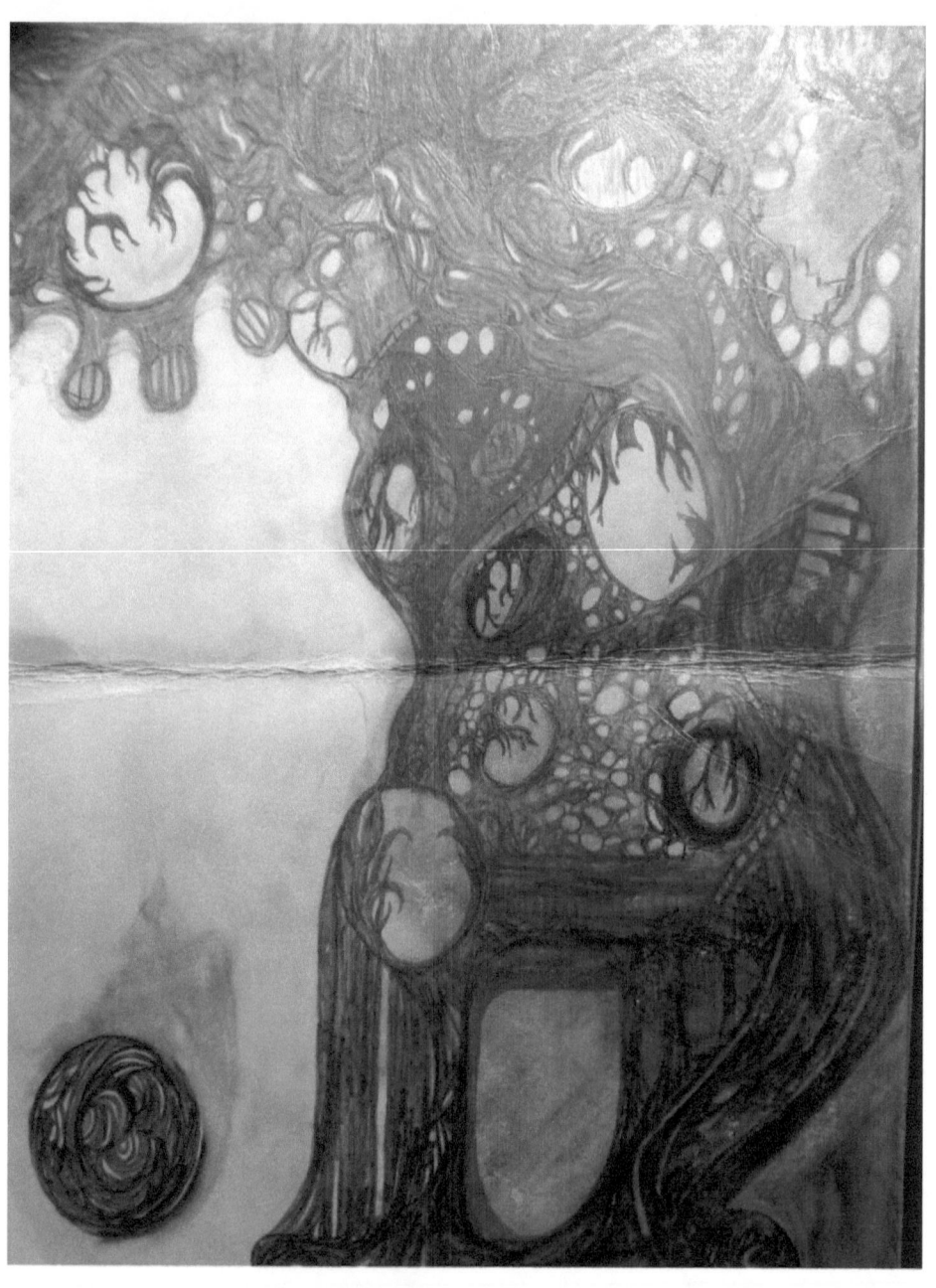

When their little legs
Start to run
And the embers

Are burning down to one
The fur on their little
Brown bodies
All singed
The limbs on their
Frame carry unhinged
Their eyes so glassy
Like little enamel beads
Start the anxious
Impervious pleadings
Cry they know will not
Be heard
Or answered this
Life or way beyond
So helpless they lie
Down their heads
To die
Just as the snow
Is starting to fly

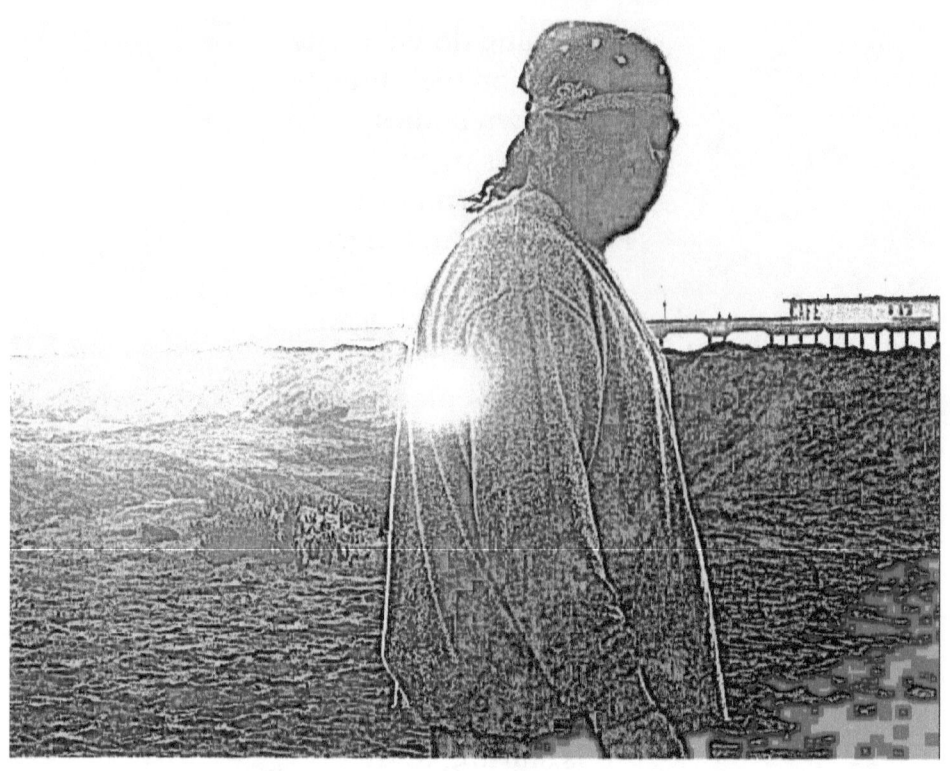

Softly wander
Away from you
Quickly we cross
Paths again
As we aimlessly
Create new
Roads to run away
From each other
Again

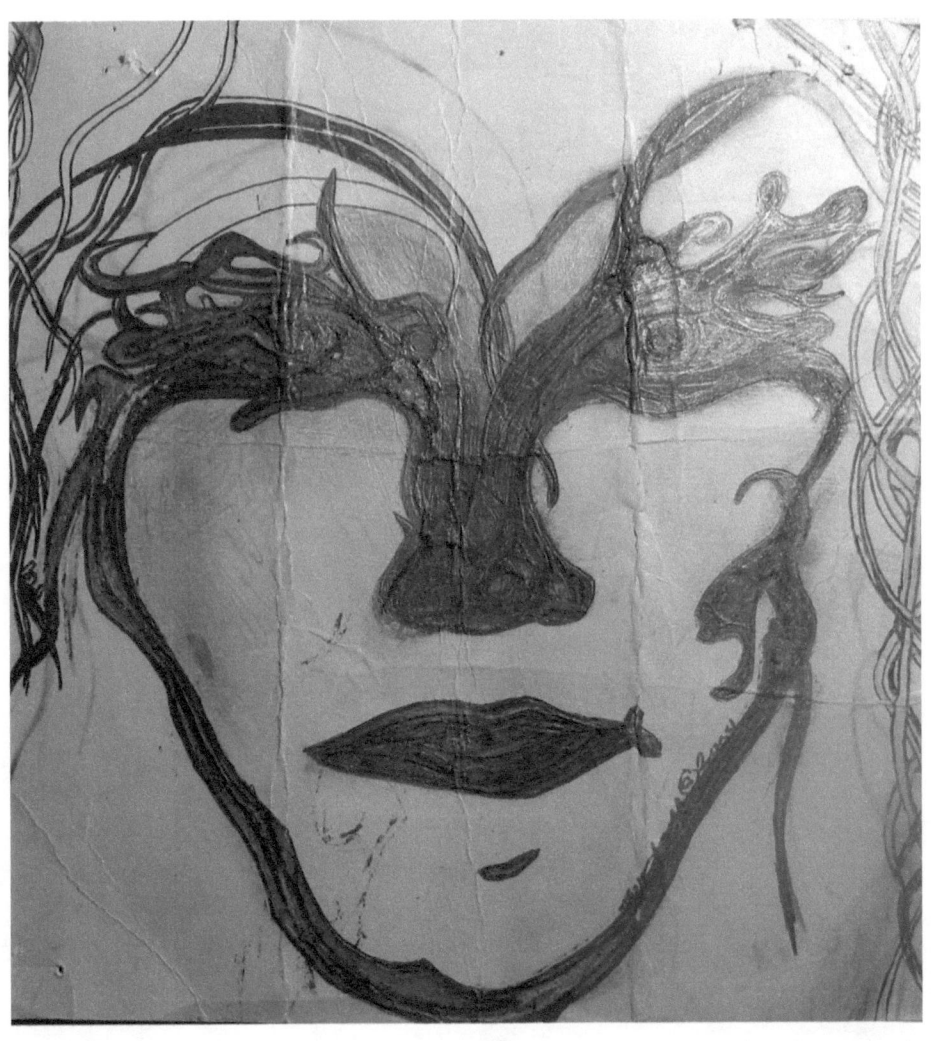

Face the fact
Paint that bitch black
And if that didn't work
Just put the shirt
Up over her head

And a window
To look out of
While you sit
In it

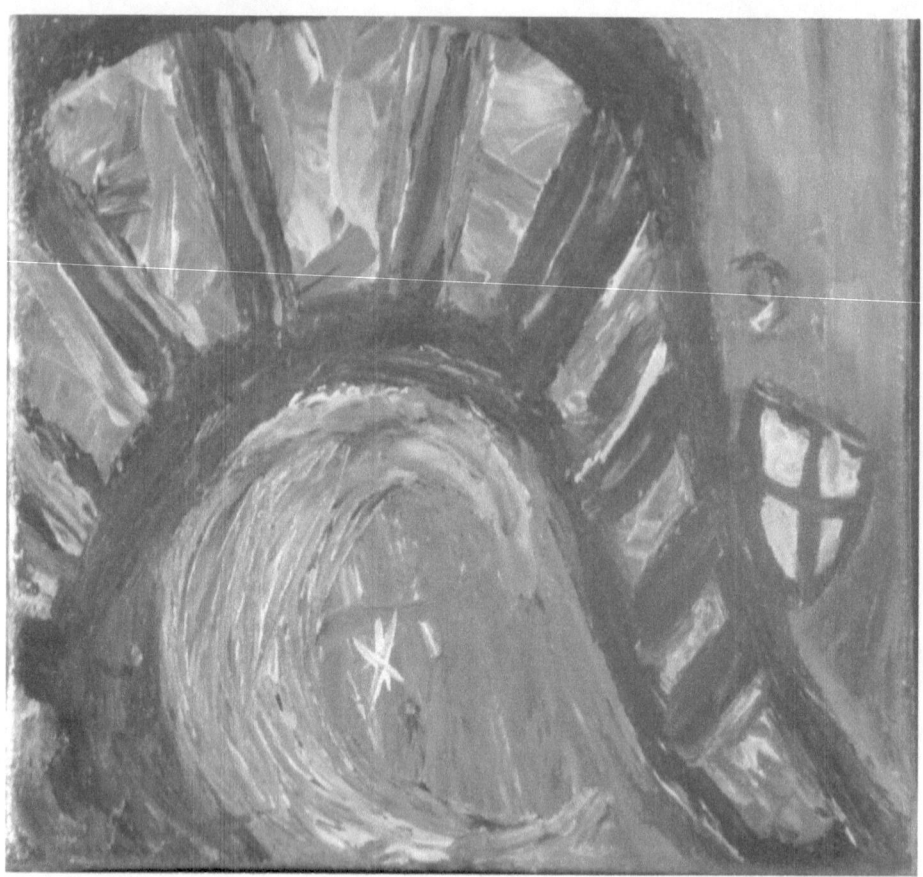

Only waiting, silent debating
Keeps me in my room
One night makes up all we are
One hour extends our life
One moment makes it all worthwhile
One time for us to do again
Pinpoint the moment
When the world changed
And you don't begin to begin
To remember just what happened
There and what was the end

It's come
The time to prepare
The time to find the perfect
Host to mother me
I can feel him out there sniffing
Somehow he knows what I'm
Thinking
Somehow he knows
I'm coming back

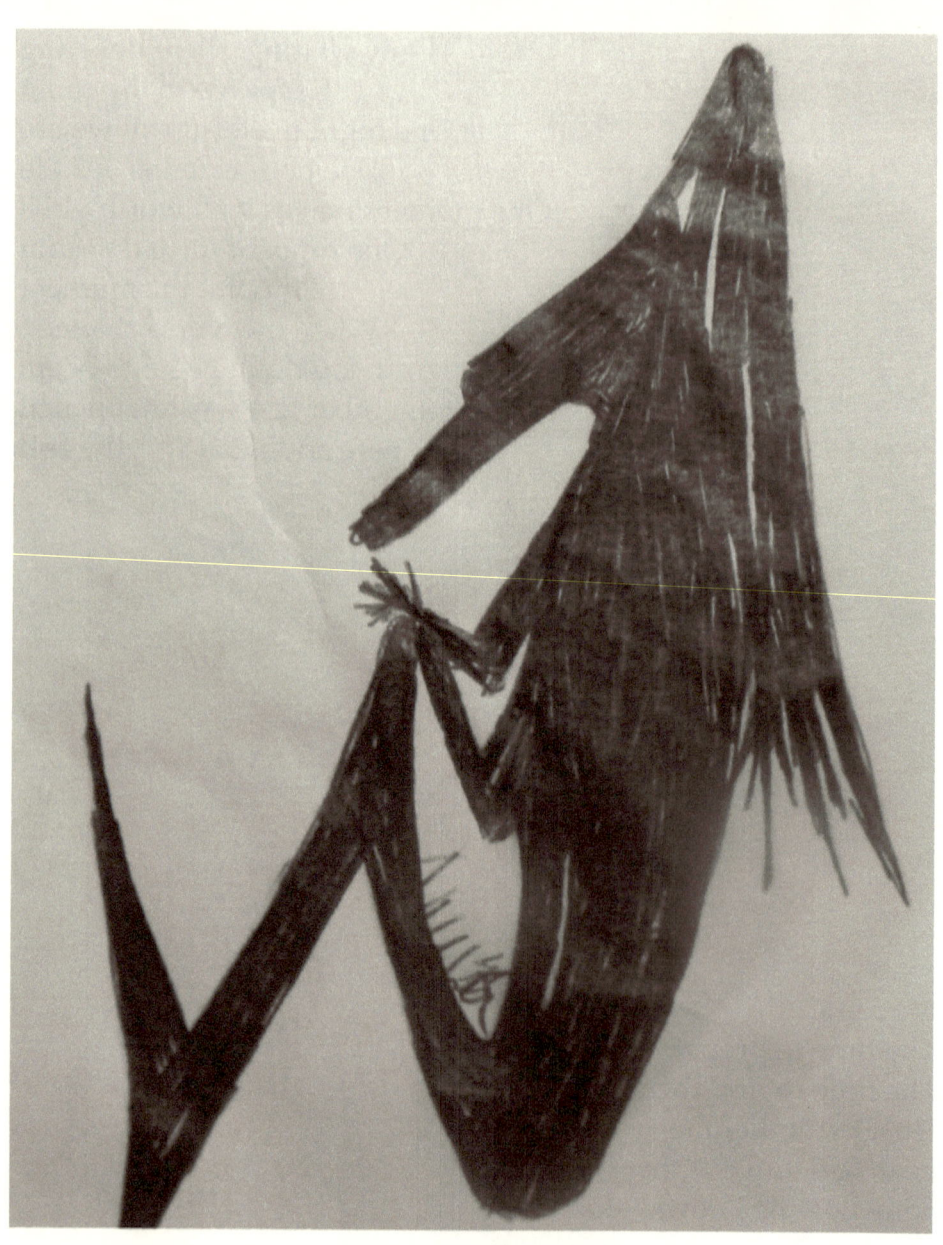

Only a moment ago
Quietly surviving
Only a moment ago
Alive

Opening quietly
The eyes in
The dark
Sitting patiently
Waiting until
You pass by
Sometimes every night
Maybe this time
He'll introduce himself

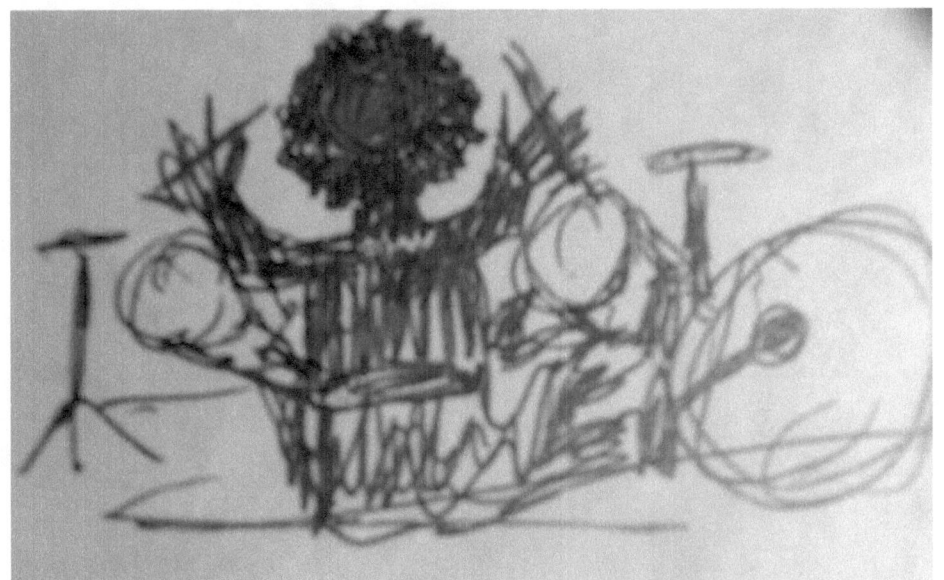

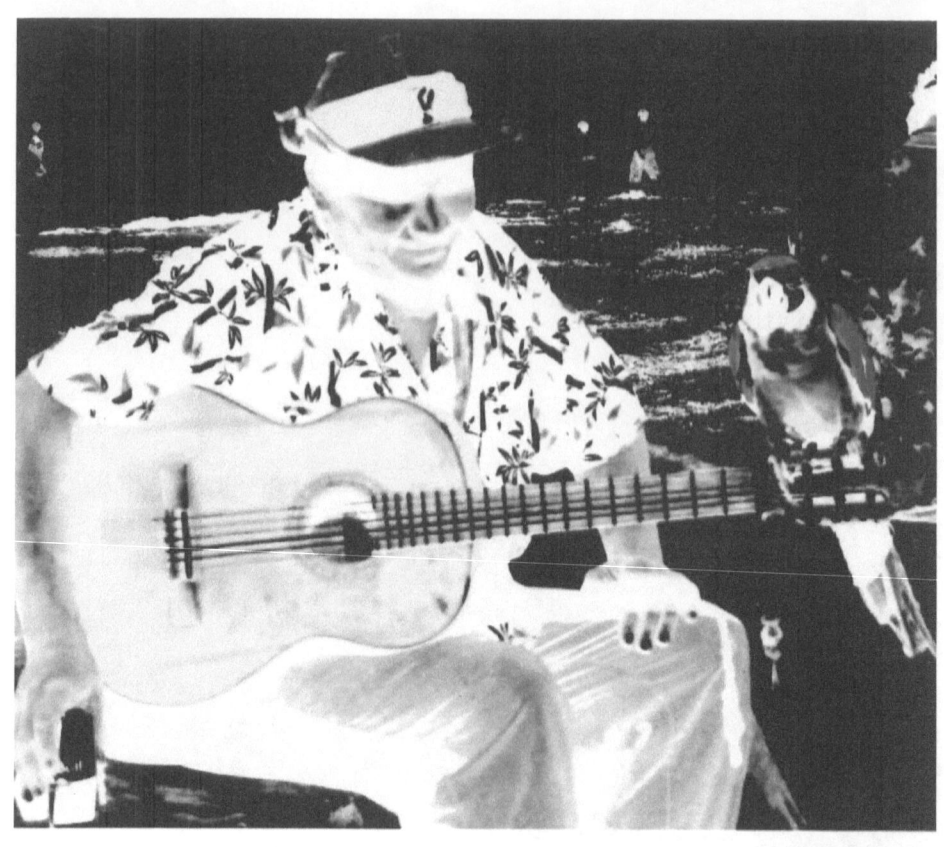

Maybe you can take
A little piece of me
Somewhere safe
Somewhere free
And let me ride
On wings and fly
Away to another
Body

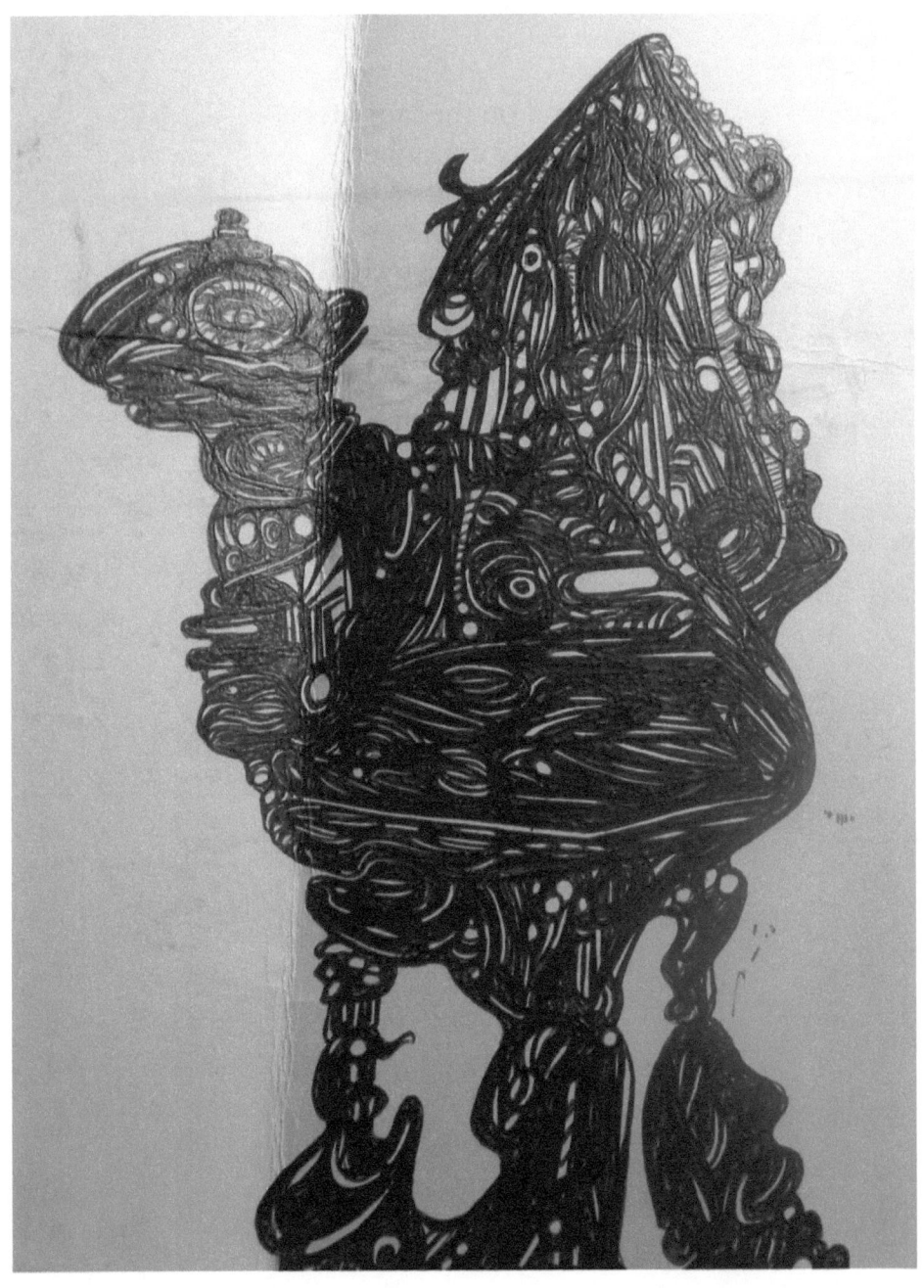

On and on the laughter
Grows and when
The sun shines the
Feeling shows
All the good you feel today
This is such a crazy
Mess
Of everything
We have to say
To keep the anger
Deep inside I guess
This way we won't
Need to hide
One another from
Ourselves and pray
Each day
We will see no
More urns on the
Mantle each night

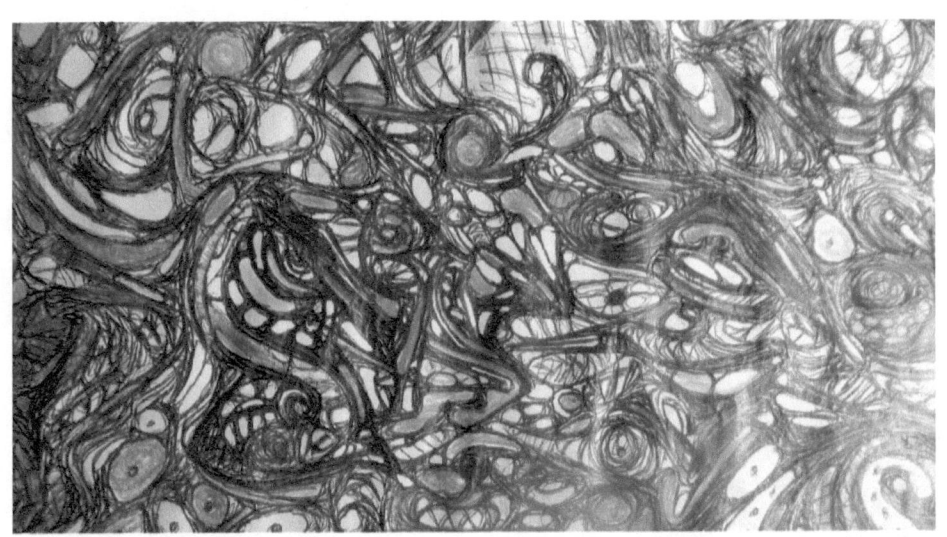

And on and on
And together again
Here we take
Everything we can
Away
To a new time and space
Where love isn't
Called a lie

Another day in paradise
So much time to get it right
Before the sun goes down

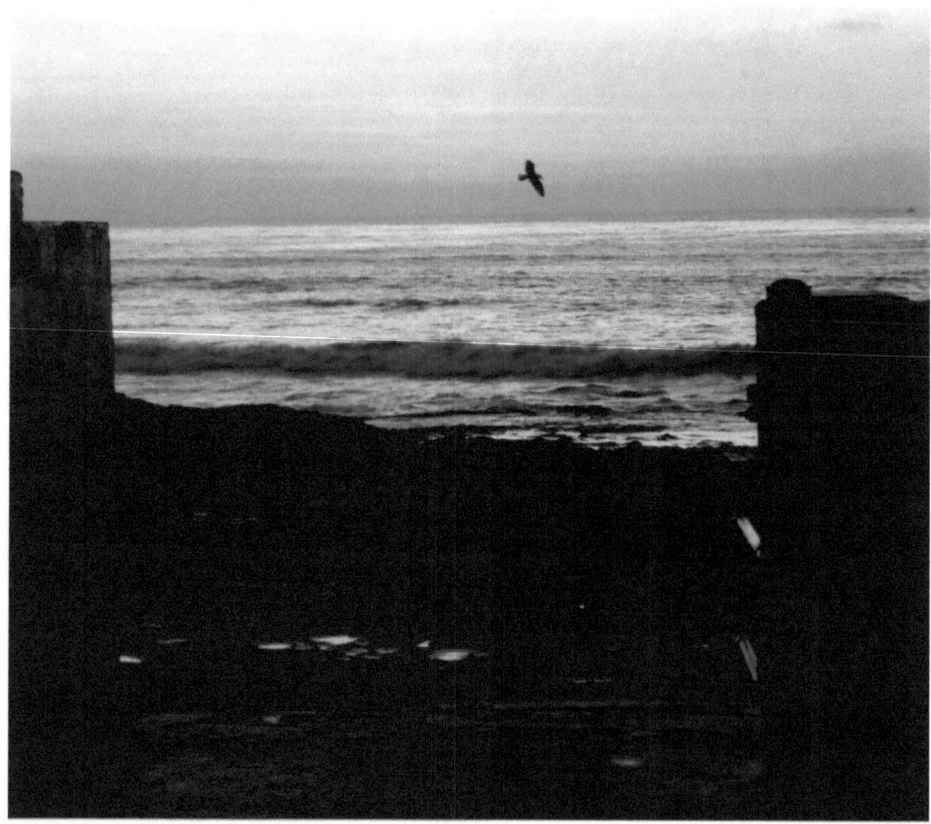

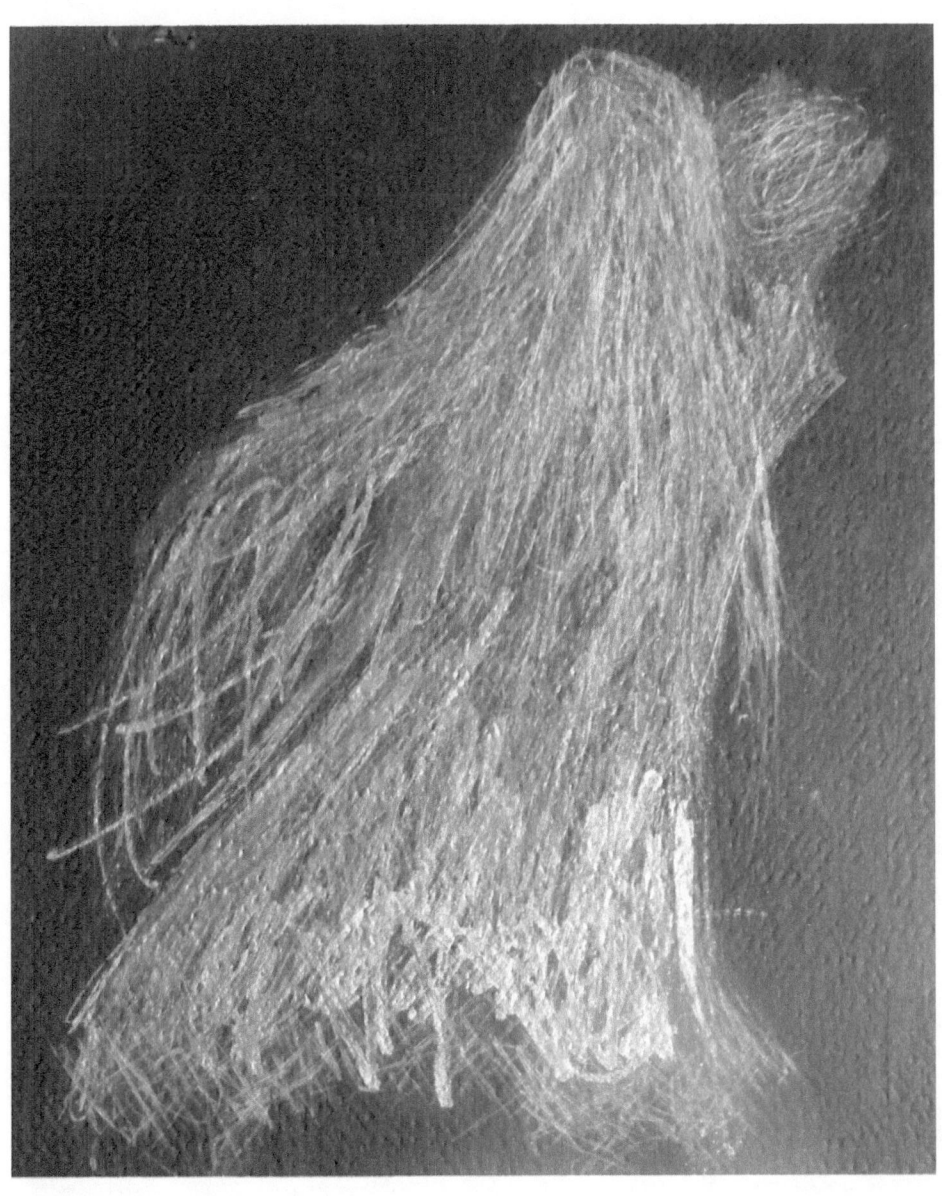

Turn around and close your
Eyes
Send the evening lullabies
To all the little ones every where
Whose beds are cold and lonely
Crystal blue shaded blinds
Cover all the windows
In a home where nothing dwells
And hope the time
Going forward never looking back
Upon the days that frighten

I dread their panting, heavy,
Telluric breath, skinless bones
Viscera creaking and fetid with
Black grease drool
How can I endure in the midst
Of this foul concentration of diesel
Genitals and the turbine driven vaginas
The ignorant throats that
Only had flamed, steamed, and hissed
And might again this very night

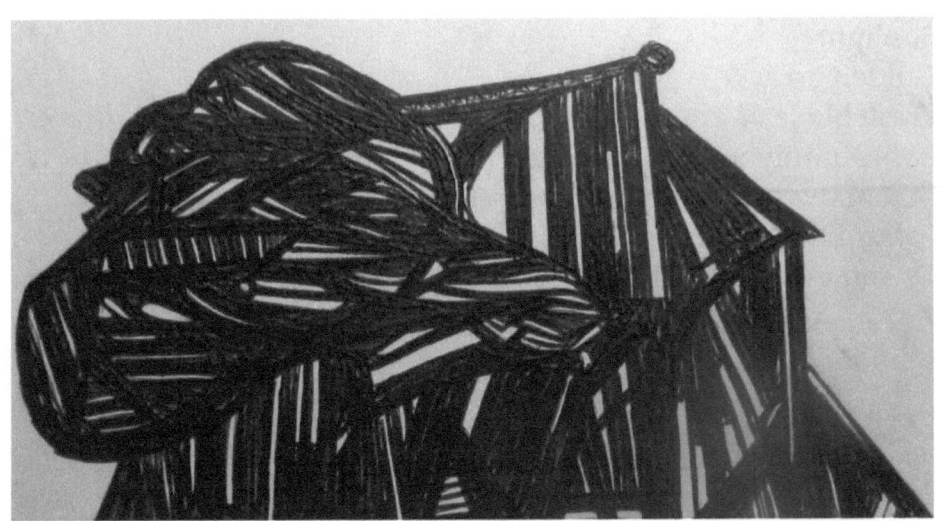

Hopeful forgetting
Of another day
That is no more
Living to remember
Things that have
Shaped me
Careful debating
Every moment
In between

Sunlight
Golden on a
Fresh blade of grass
Forever only in one moment
Before the sun moves away
Behind the clouds
Or somewhere else

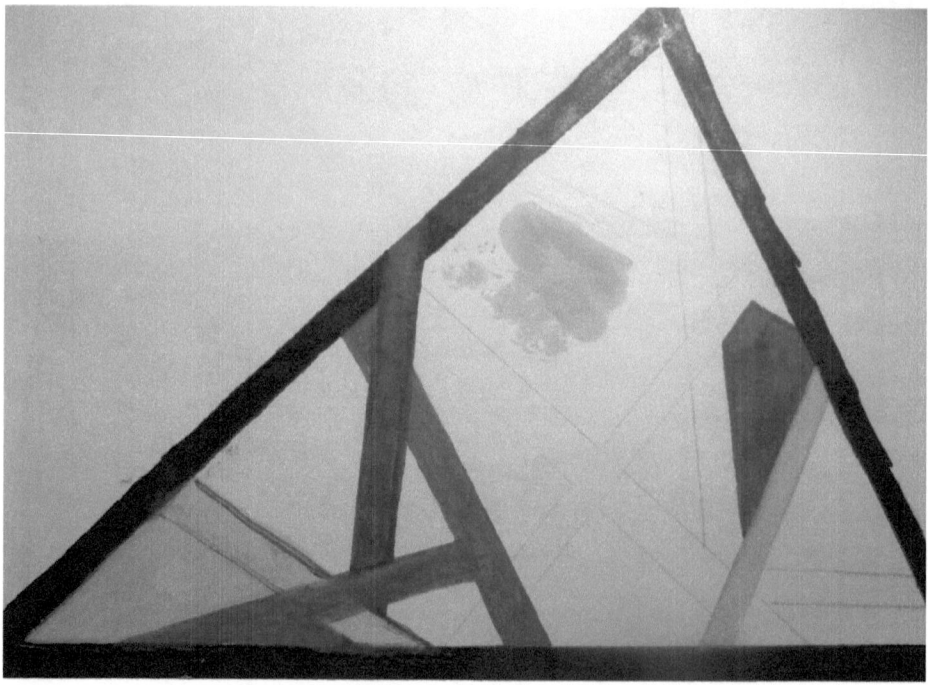

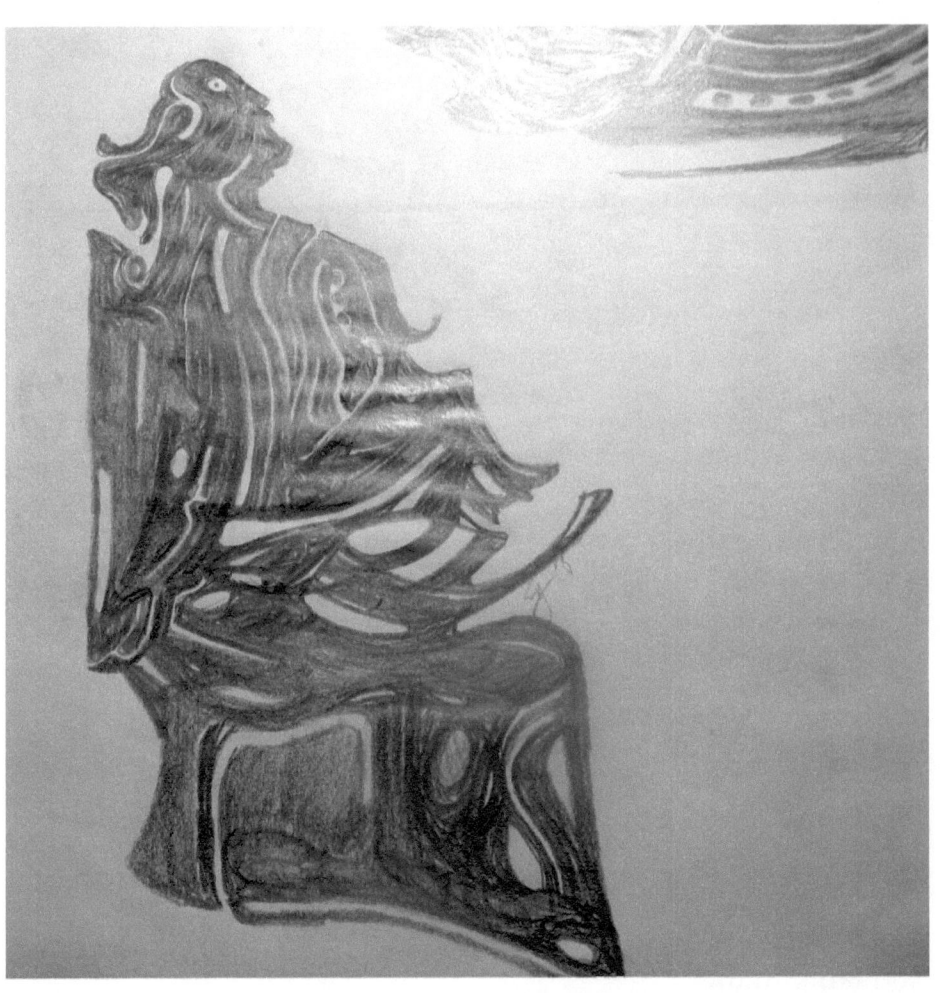

Last night you said that it maybe
Time for a new place, a new face
The distance close to the furthest corner
Of your mind
Where you and I
Could finally go alone with no overkill

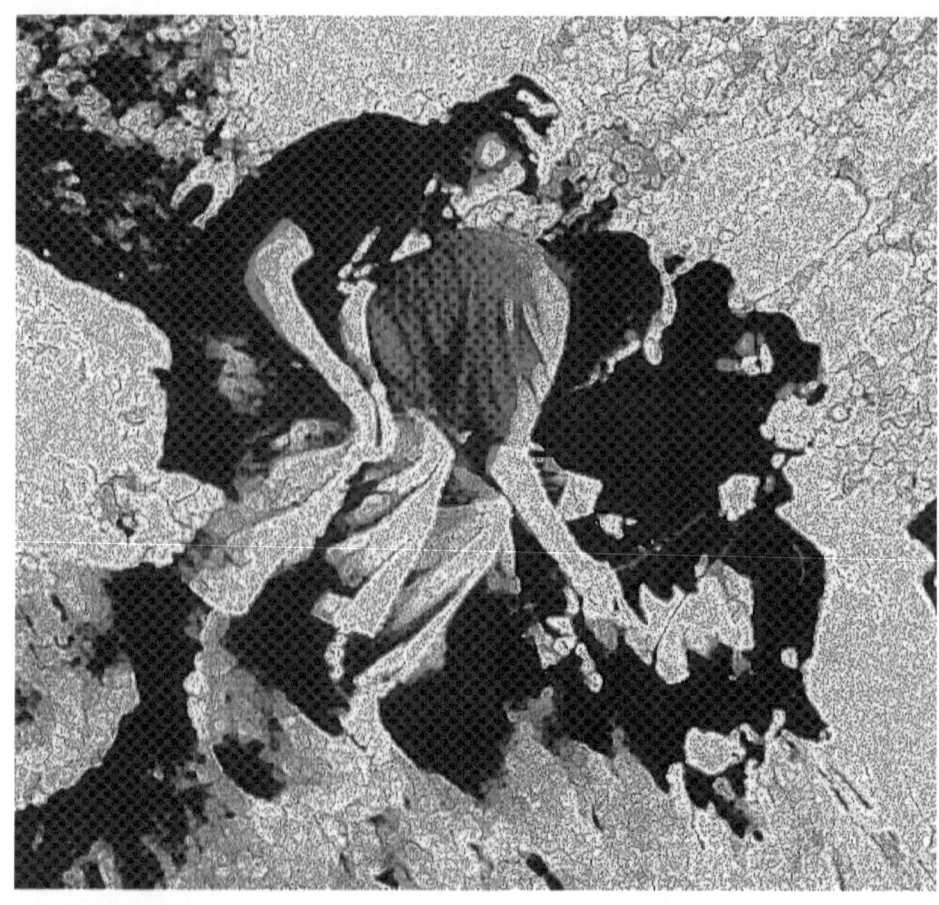

When will it all begin to crumble
And fall into the
Rubble of decay?
How long can we continue on
To convince everyone
That it's all under control
How long will the fear go on
That the truth will tell the lie

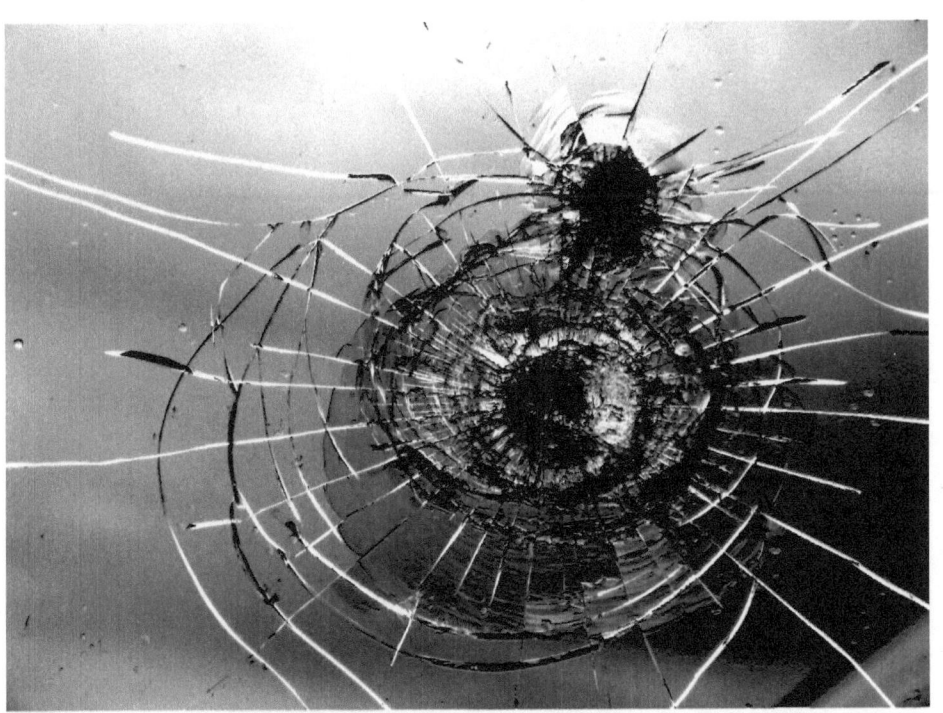

Sisters won't you entertain
The notion of something new
Take a shiny penny
It could be real soon
To fall from your lap
To a brand new world
That will resuscitate your
Mind and make your dreams
New adventures

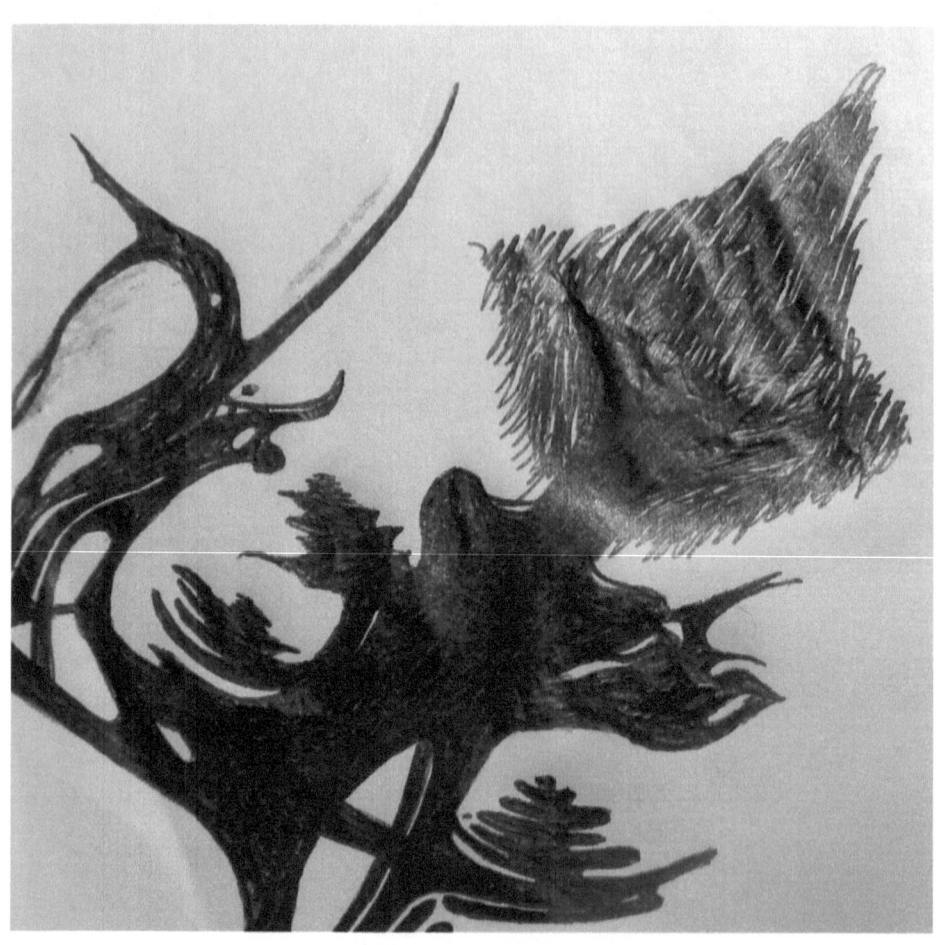

On and on
And on
The waves
Keep crashing
And pushing the sands
Away from all the demons
We hide
Away deep under the
Surface

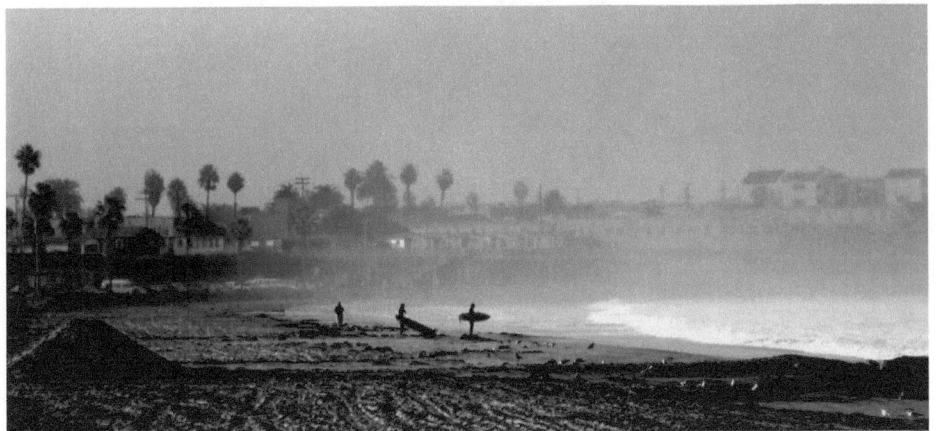

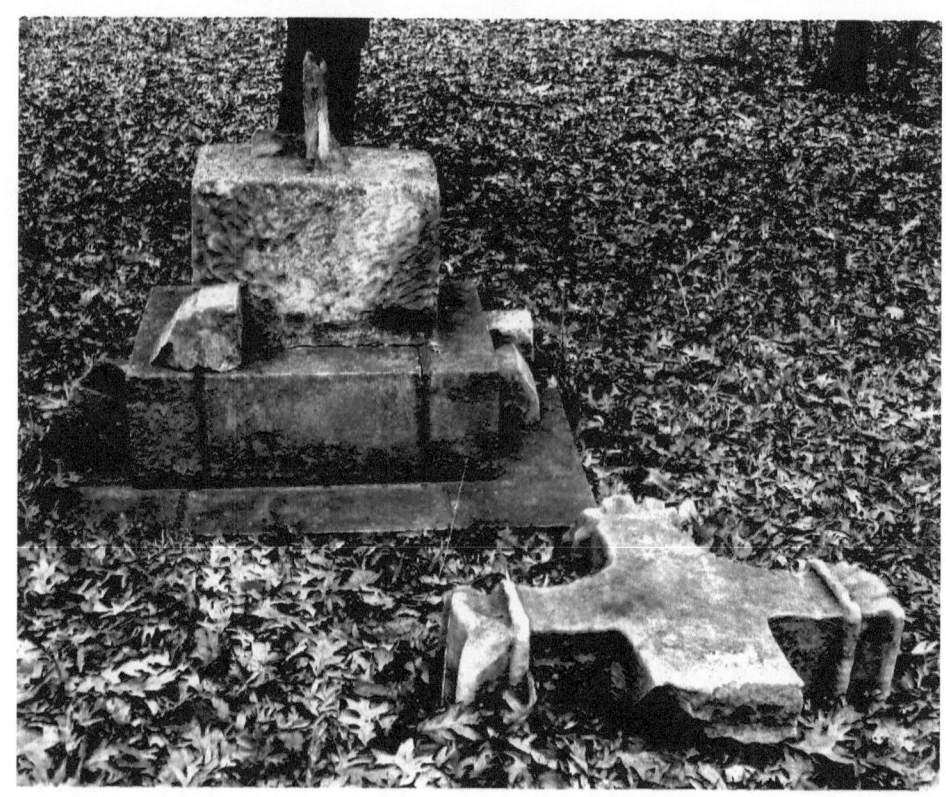

Walk alone
Looking maybe
Single lane
Lonely path
Going home stupid
Today Tomorrow
Talk alone
Thinking nothing
Okay today
No more tomorrow

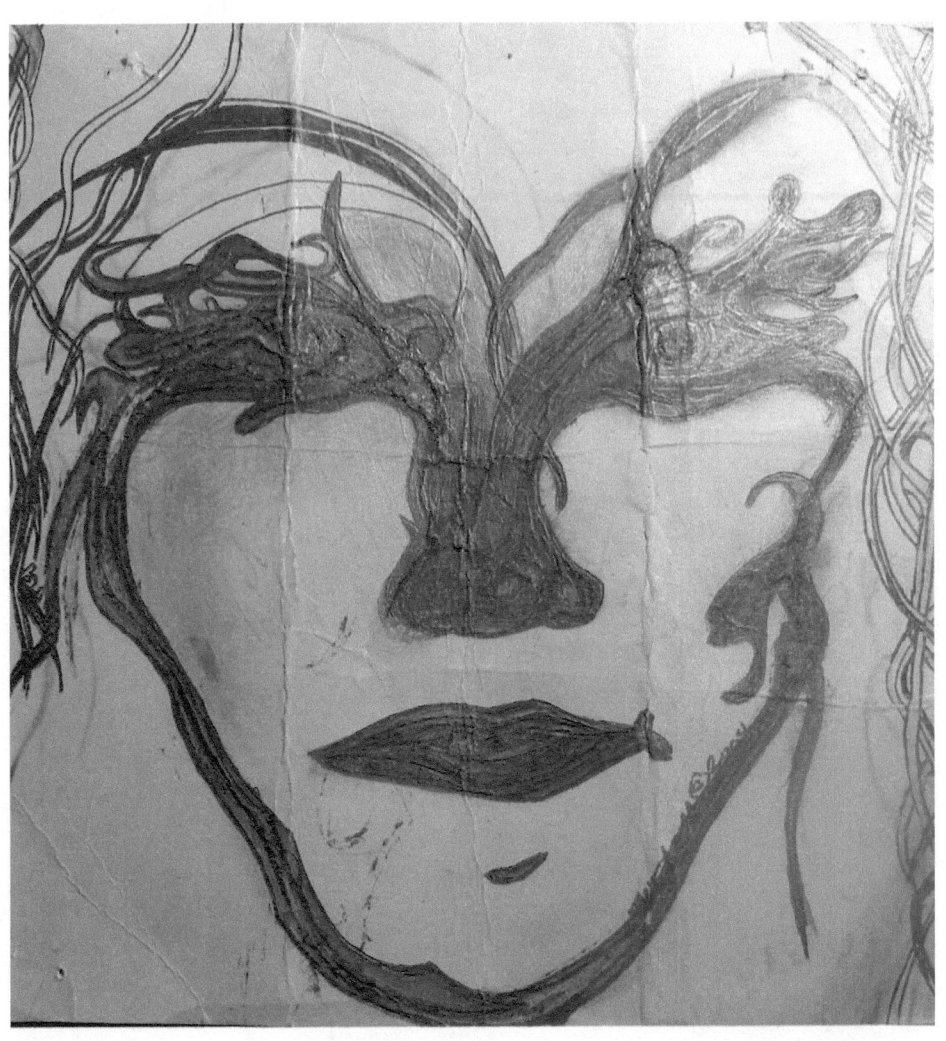

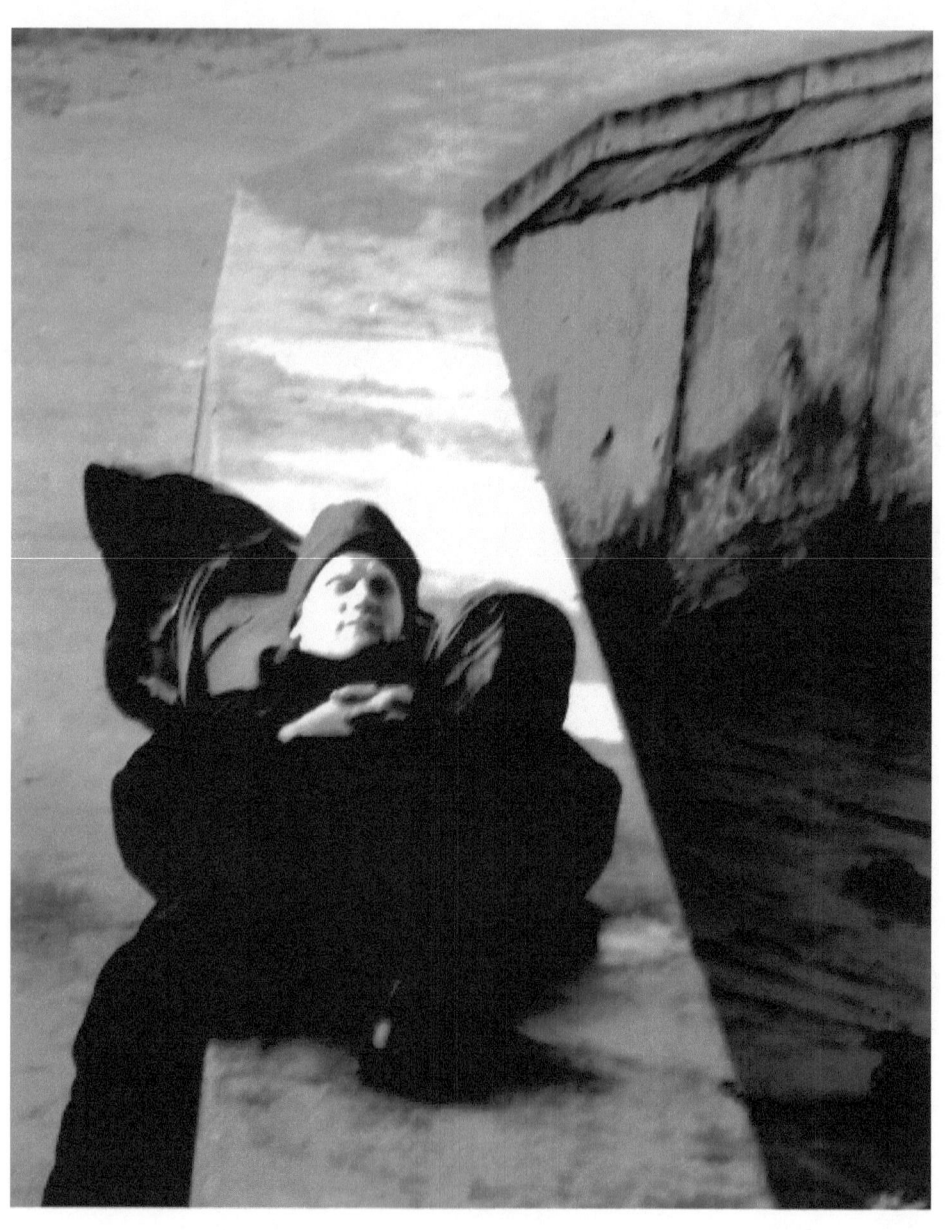

Sitting in special place
Take a breath
And feel the shine
On your face

As you get a space
Within your troubled mind
Easily amused by simple
Things that take away the
Pain placing yourself in
Another land giving yourself
A reason to keep going on
In life through even the last season

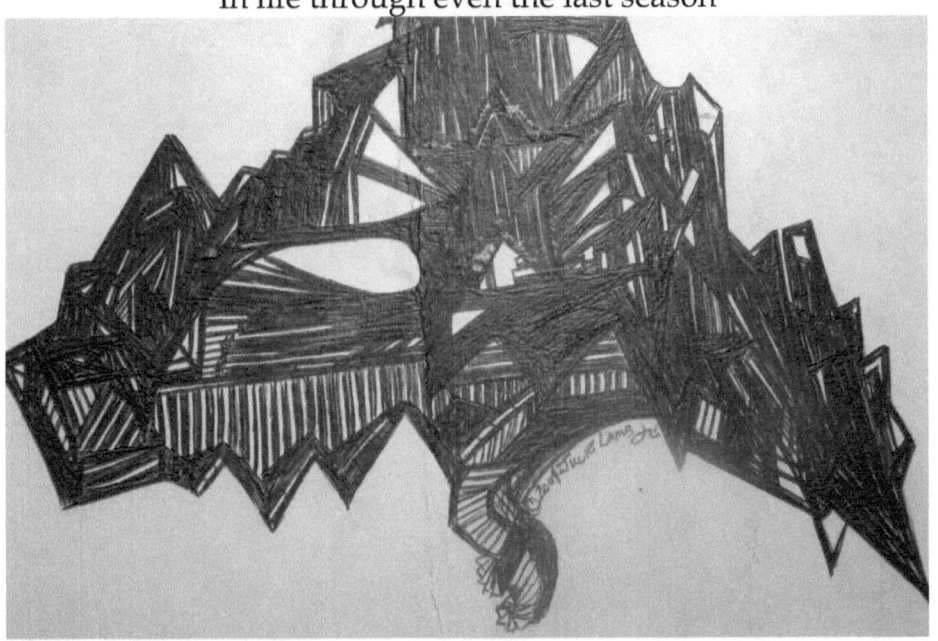

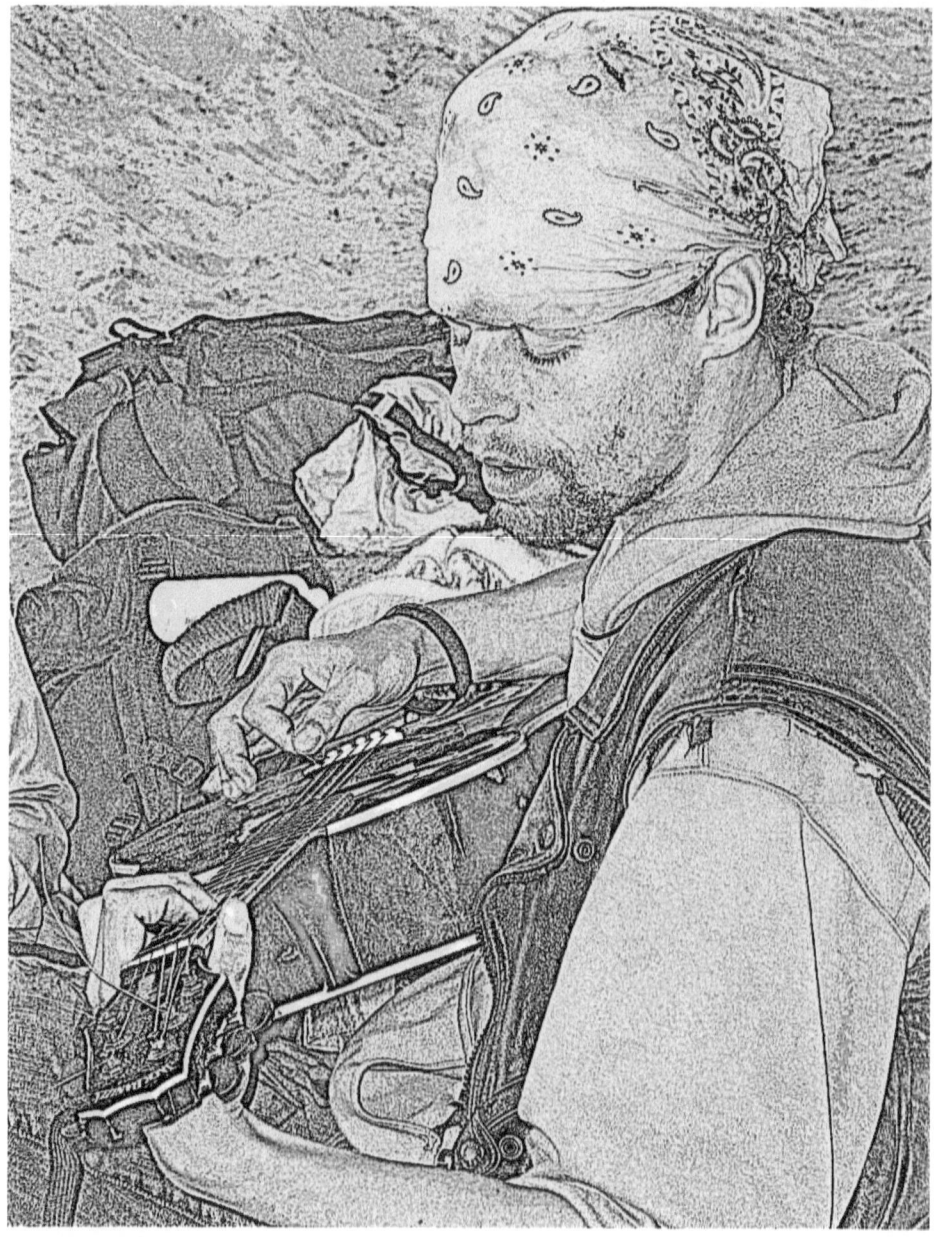

Under a blue
Umbrella
Stands an old dark
Man
Among the wanderers
Running to and fro' in
Search of something
Anything to make them
Feel alive

Well
Here I sit again
Wondering where you are
I heard your van again
Leaving again
So I guess I had to really know
Before I said goodbye
To you forever
Tomorrow when I wake
Really early
To catch the bus for the
Walk in court
Since I was late for the curb

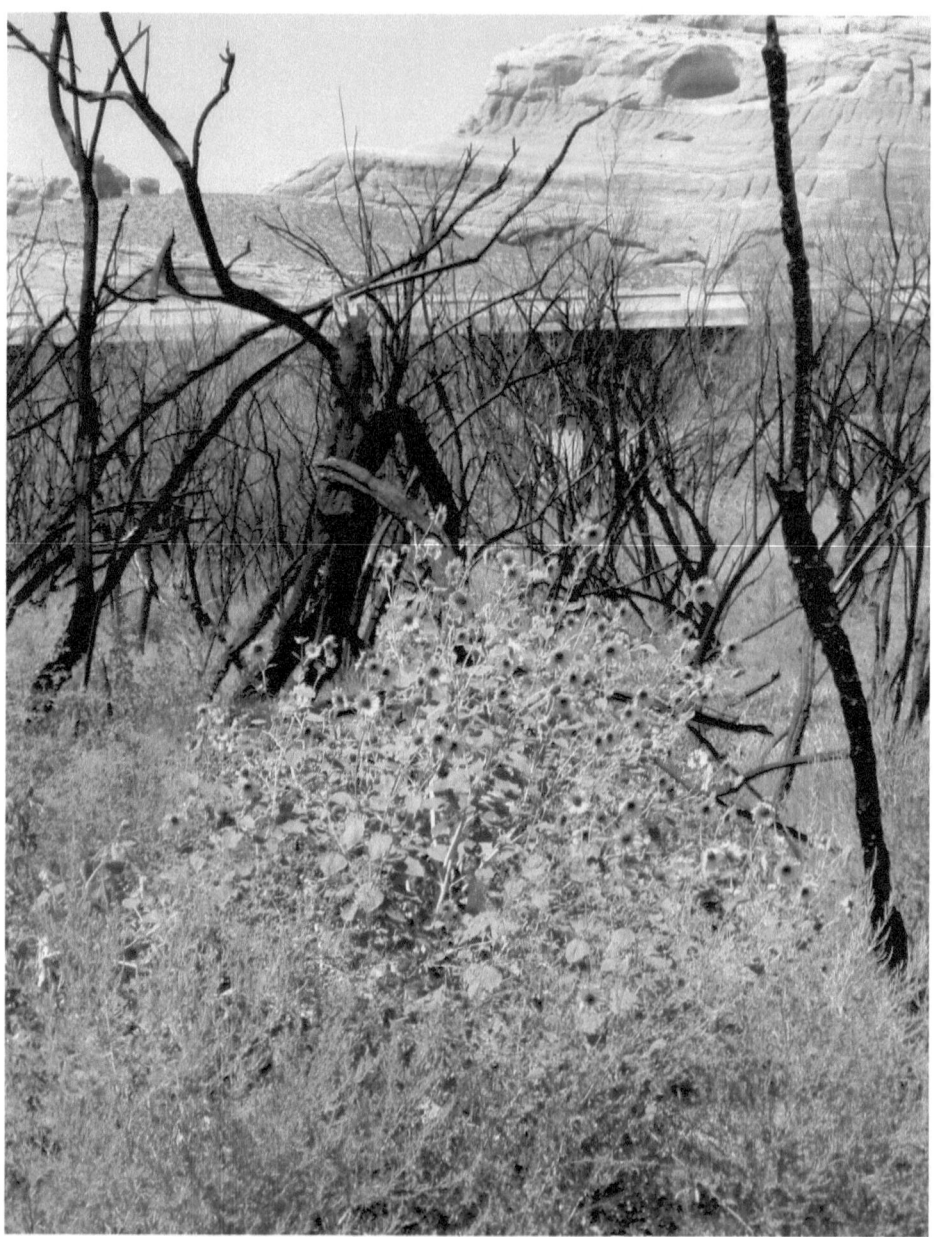

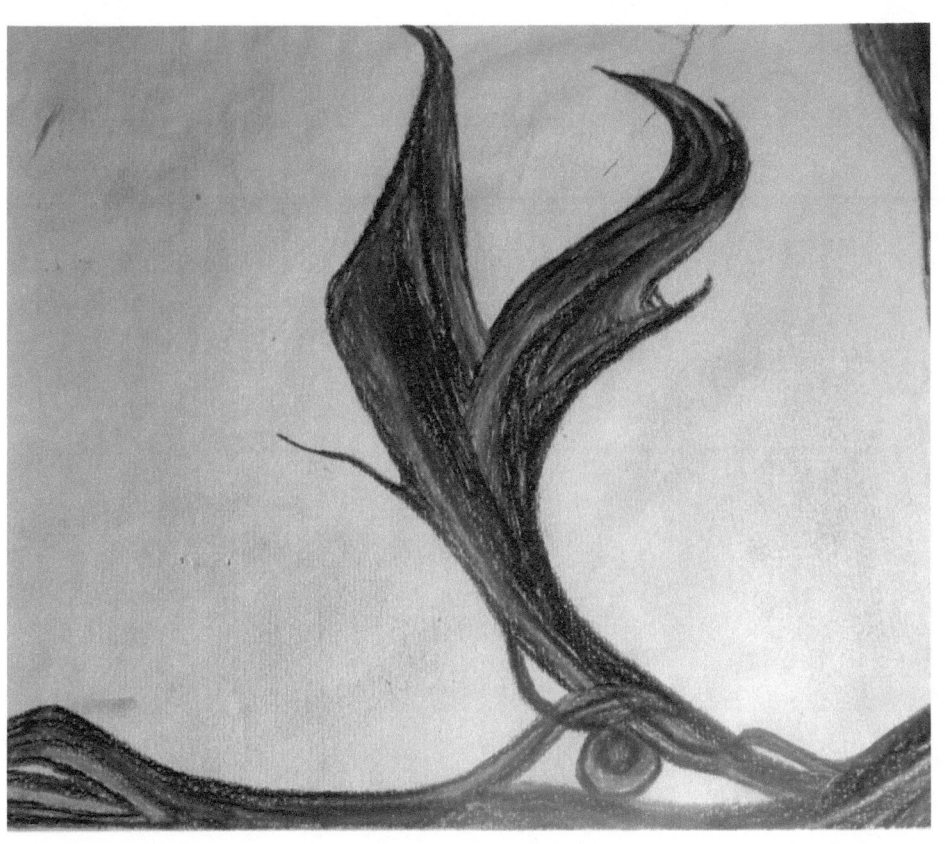

Am I the only one?
Do you feel connected?
Do you hear what I'm thinking?
And is it a voice in your ear
Or a sound in your head?
Can you please tell me
How to make it stop?
And can you explain to me how it began?

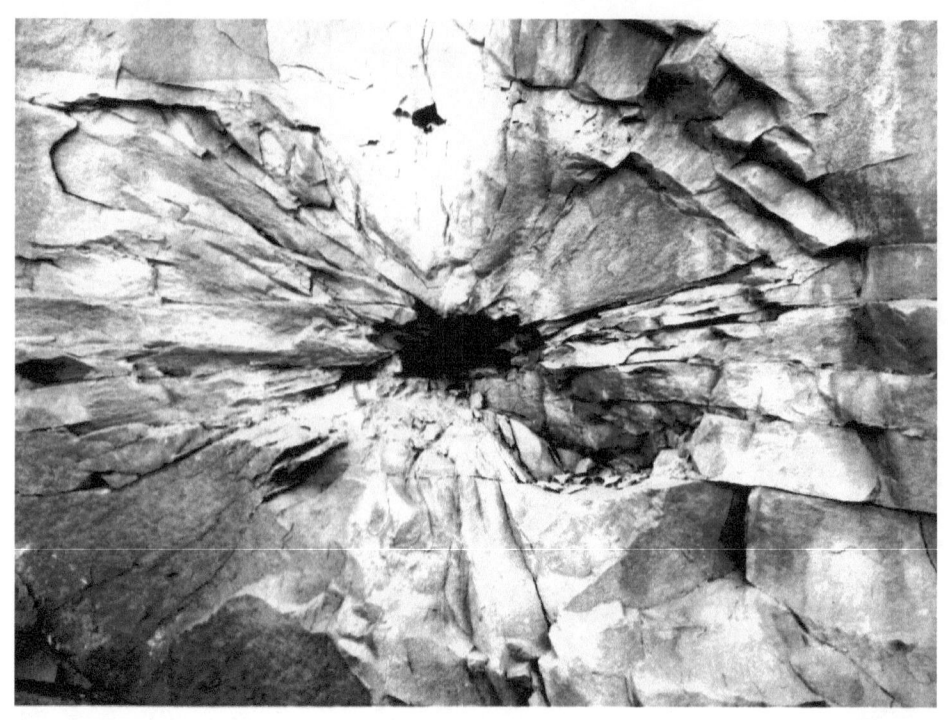

I'm a bomb
I'm on the edge
Don't push me

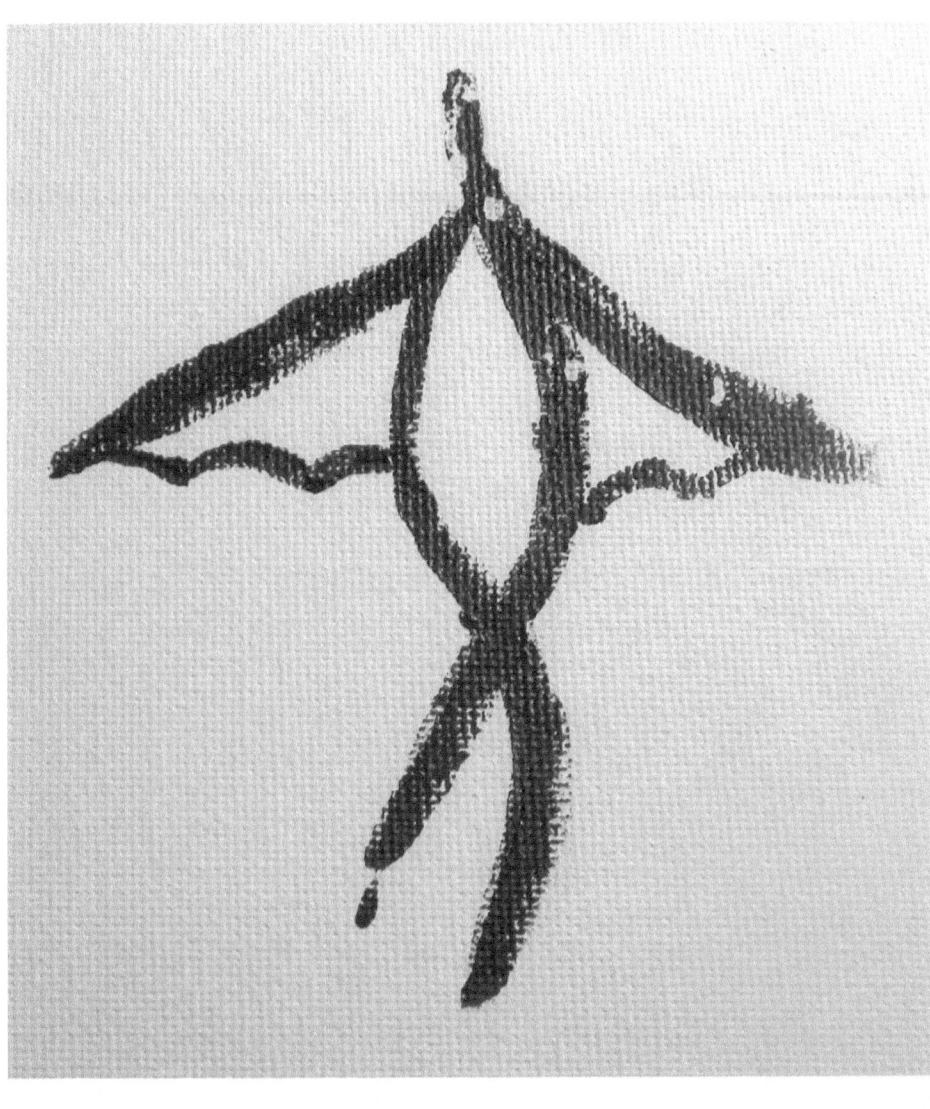

I want to live I want to live
I want to live I want to live
I have the strength to
control this urge to smoke
I want to live I want to
live I am strong I want to
live I want to live. I am
strong I want to live I want
to live I want to live I am
strong I want to live. I am good
I am strong I deserve to live I
want to live. I want to live, I
deserve a life I want to live
I am strong I am good.
I want to live
I am good I want to live I am strong
I deserve to smile I deserve to laugh
I am strong I want to live......
I am strong I want to live I want
to live I want to live I want to live
I want to live. I am strong. I
want to live.

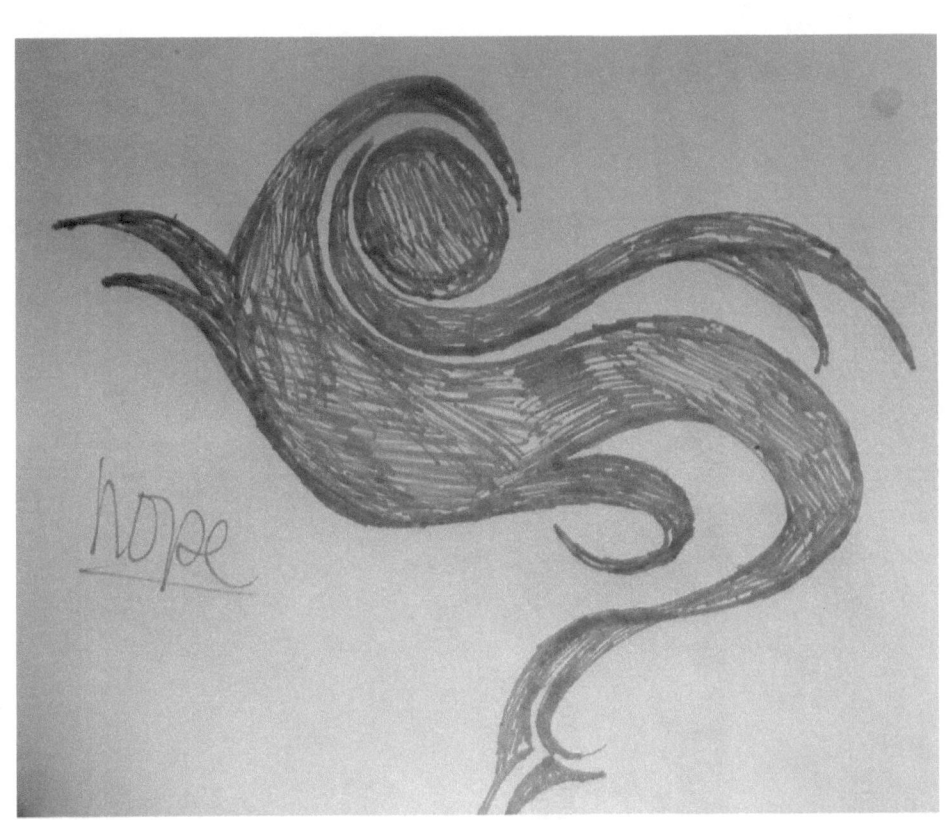

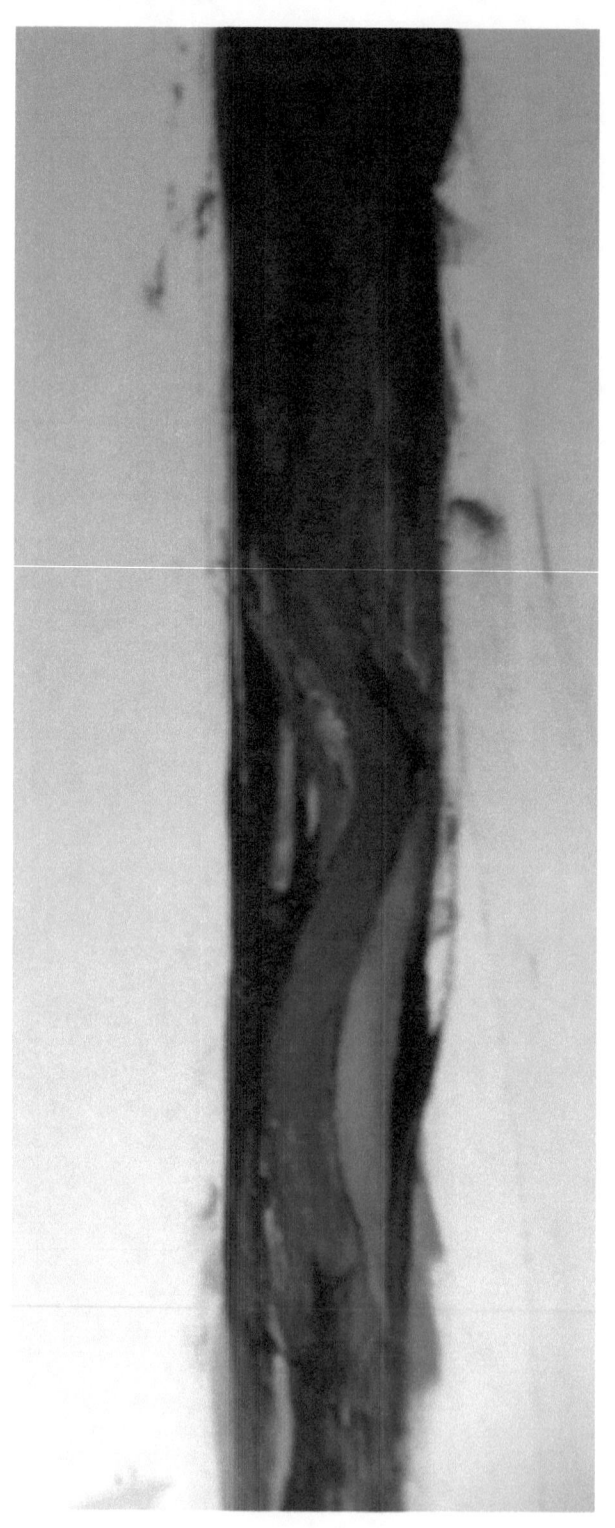

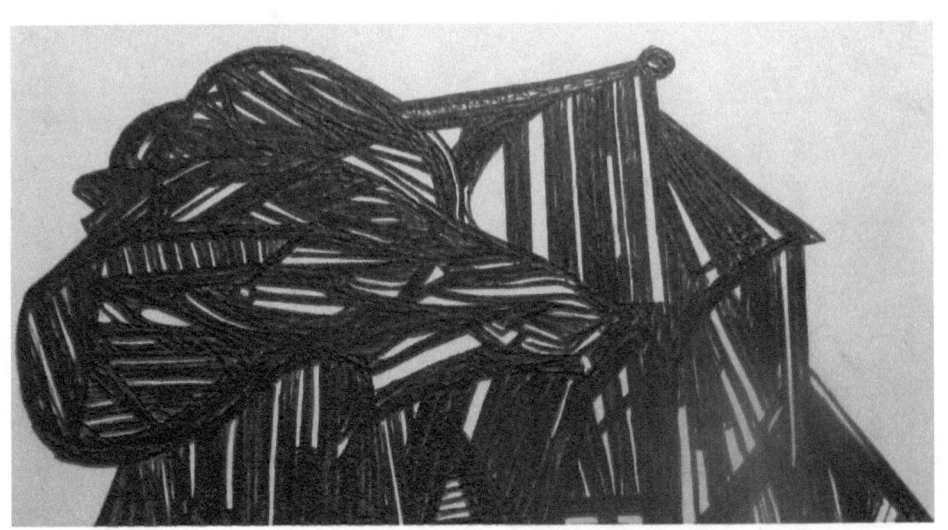

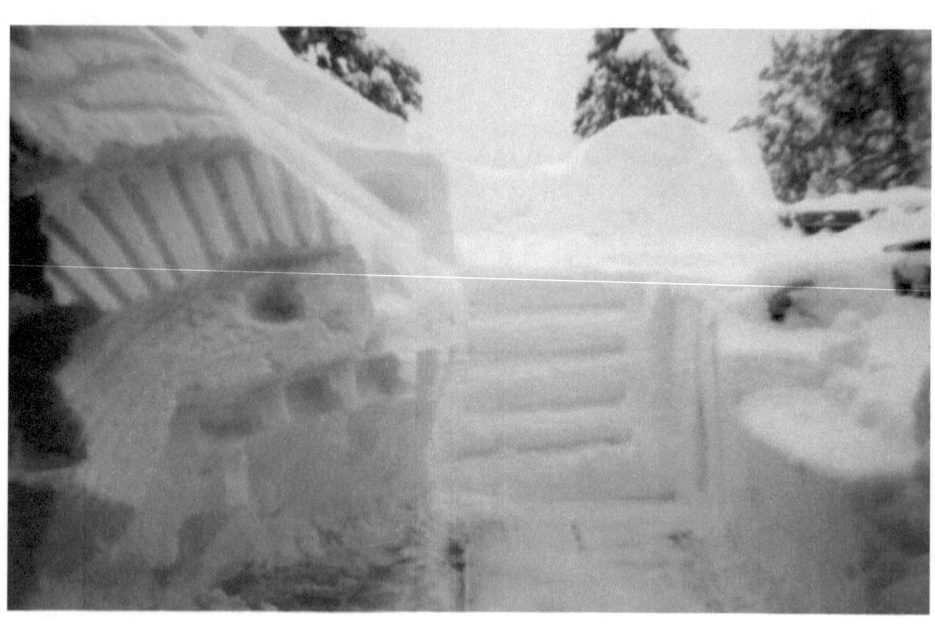

I want to live, I want to live.
I want to live, I want to live.
I will live. I will live. I will
survive this. I need to survive
this. I want to live! I
want to live. I am a good
person. I deserve to live. I
want to live I want to live.
I am a beautiful woman.
I want to live, I will live.
I will survive this. I am strong.
I am beautiful I am good.
I want to live

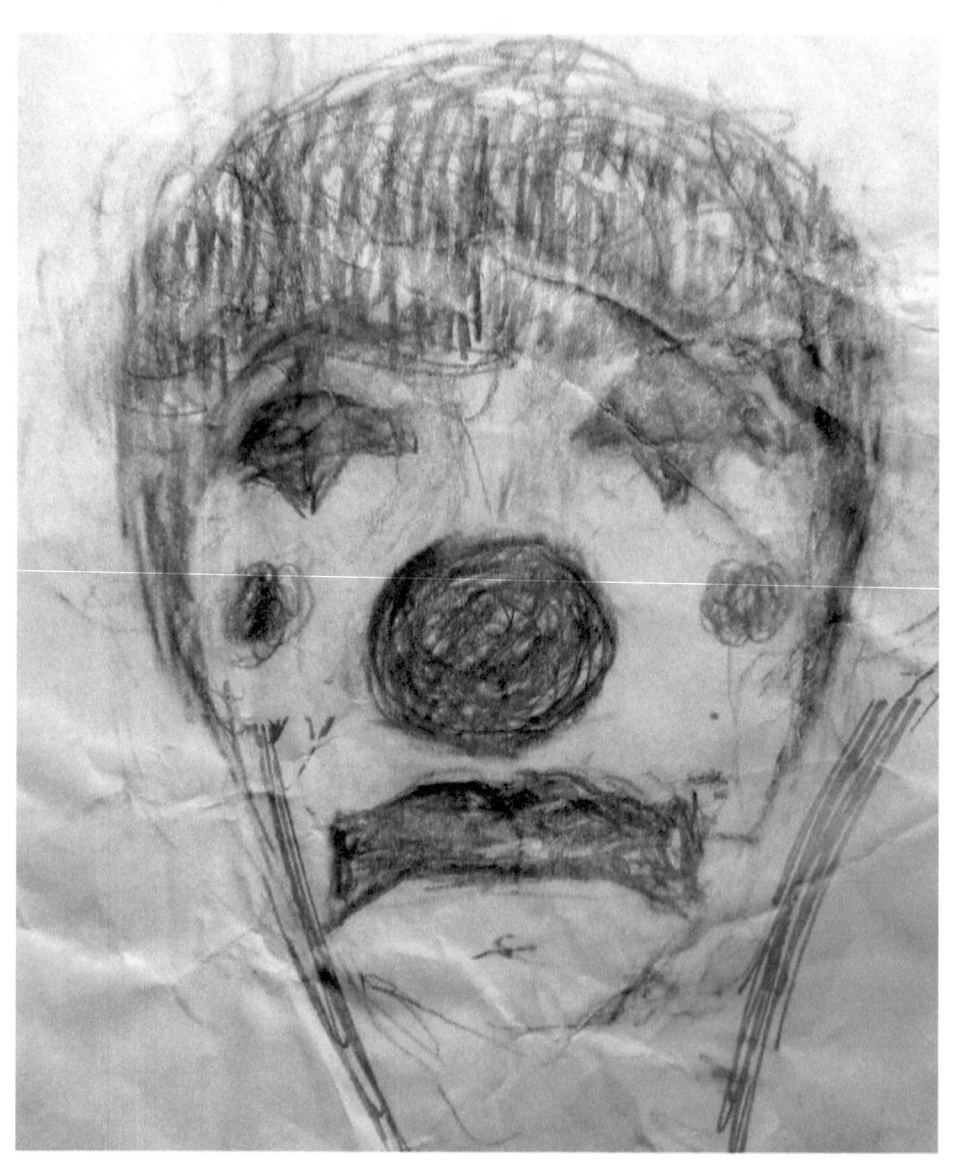

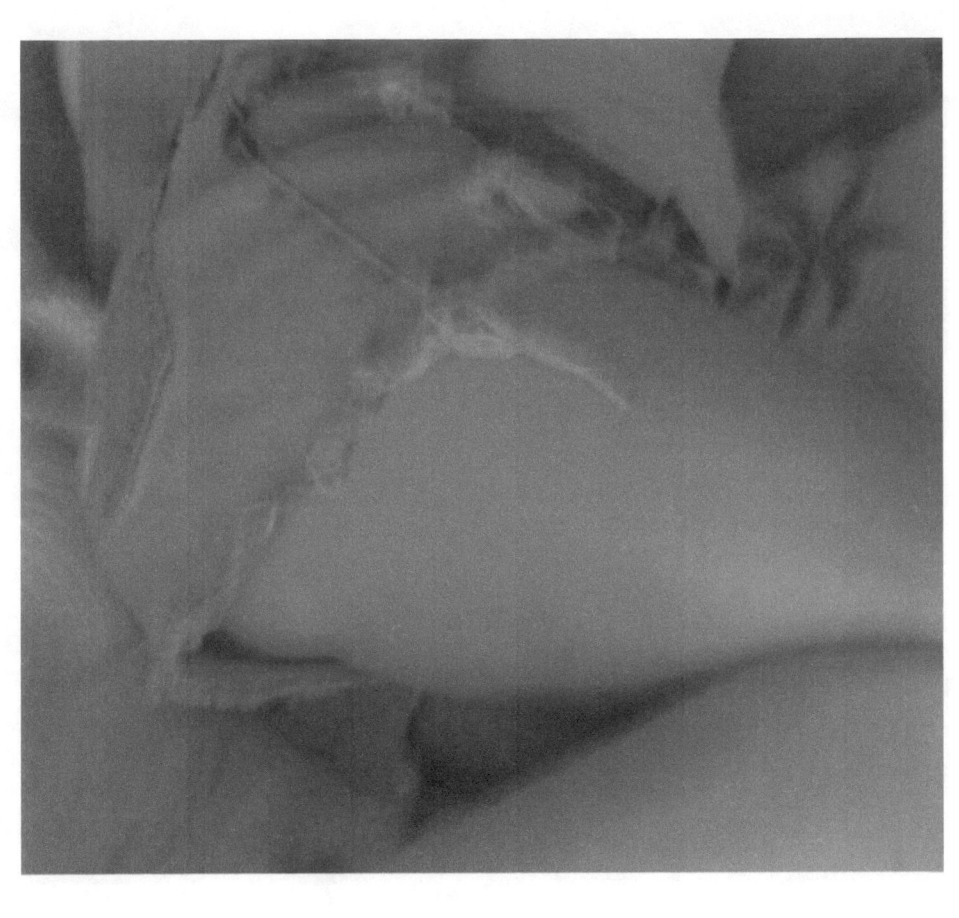

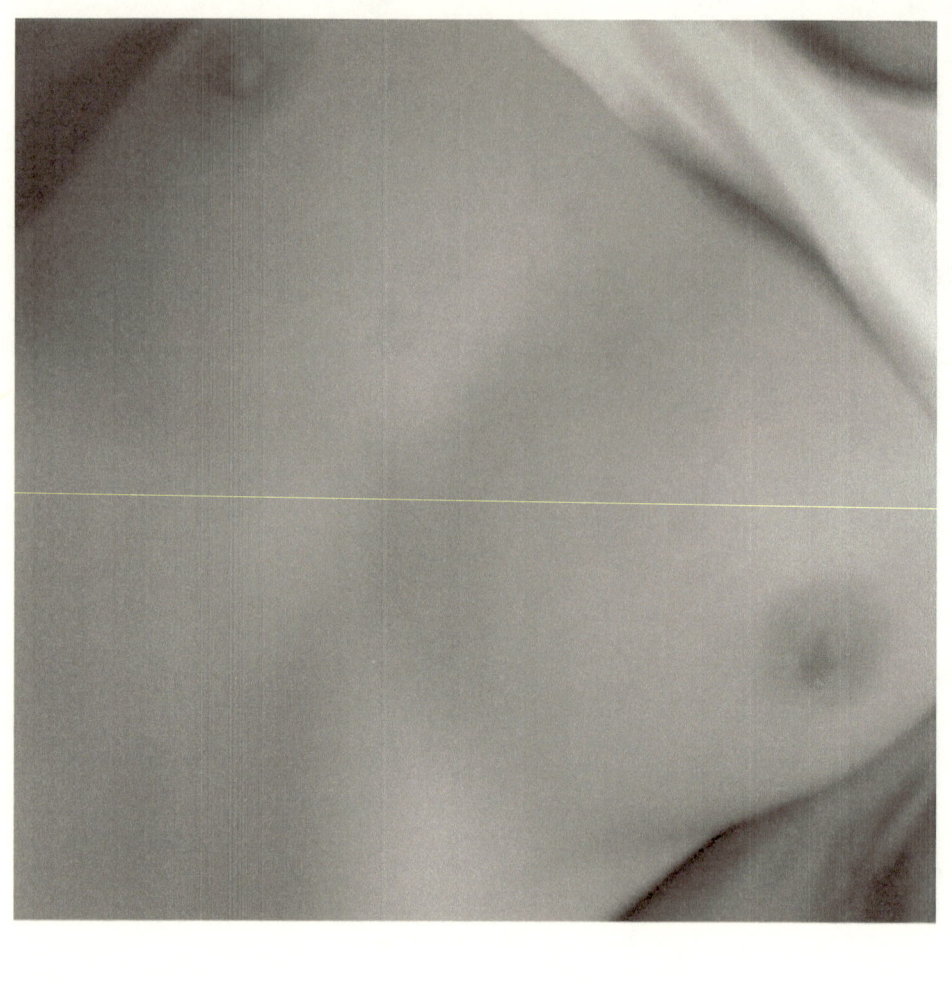

SKETCH, WRITE, CREATE

SKETCH, WRITE, CREATE

SKETCH, WRITE, CREATE

SKETCH, WRITE, CREATE

SKETCH, WRITE, CREATE

SKETCH, WRITE, CREATE

SKETCH, WRITE, CREATE

SKETCH, WRITE, CREATE

SKETCH, WRITE, CREATE

SKETCH, WRITE, CREATE

SKETCH, WRITE, CREATE

SKETCH, WRITE, CREATE

SKETCH, WRITE, CREATE

SKETCH, WRITE, CREATE

SKETCH, WRITE, CREATE

SKETCH, WRITE, CREATE

SKETCH, WRITE, CREATE

SKETCH, WRITE, CREATE

SKETCH, WRITE, CREATE

SKETCH, WRITE, CREATE

SKETCH, WRITE, CREATE

SKETCH, WRITE, CREATE

SKETCH, WRITE, CREATE

SKETCH, WRITE, CREATE

SKETCH, WRITE, CREATE

SKETCH, WRITE, CREATE

SKETCH, WRITE, CREATE

SKETCH, WRITE, CREATE

SKETCH, WRITE, CREATE

SKETCH, WRITE, CREATE

SKETCH, WRITE, CREATE

SKETCH, WRITE, CREATE

SKETCH, WRITE, CREATE

SKETCH, WRITE, CREATE

SKETCH, WRITE, CREATE

SKETCH, WRITE, CREATE

SKETCH, WRITE, CREATE

SKETCH, WRITE, CREATE